MYSTICAL

Mandalas

AN ADULT COLORING BOOK

Vol. 2

Zhena Khasha

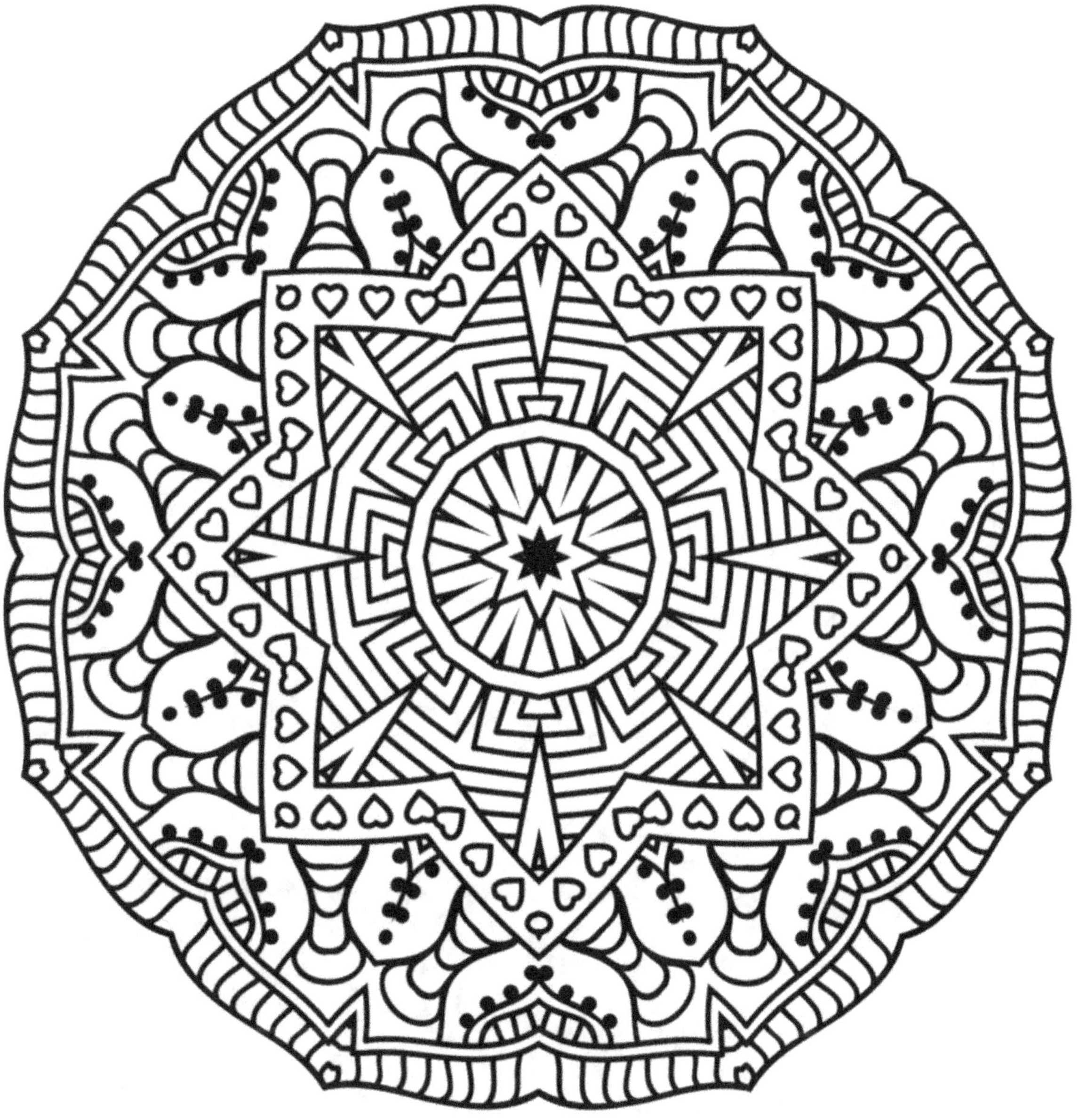

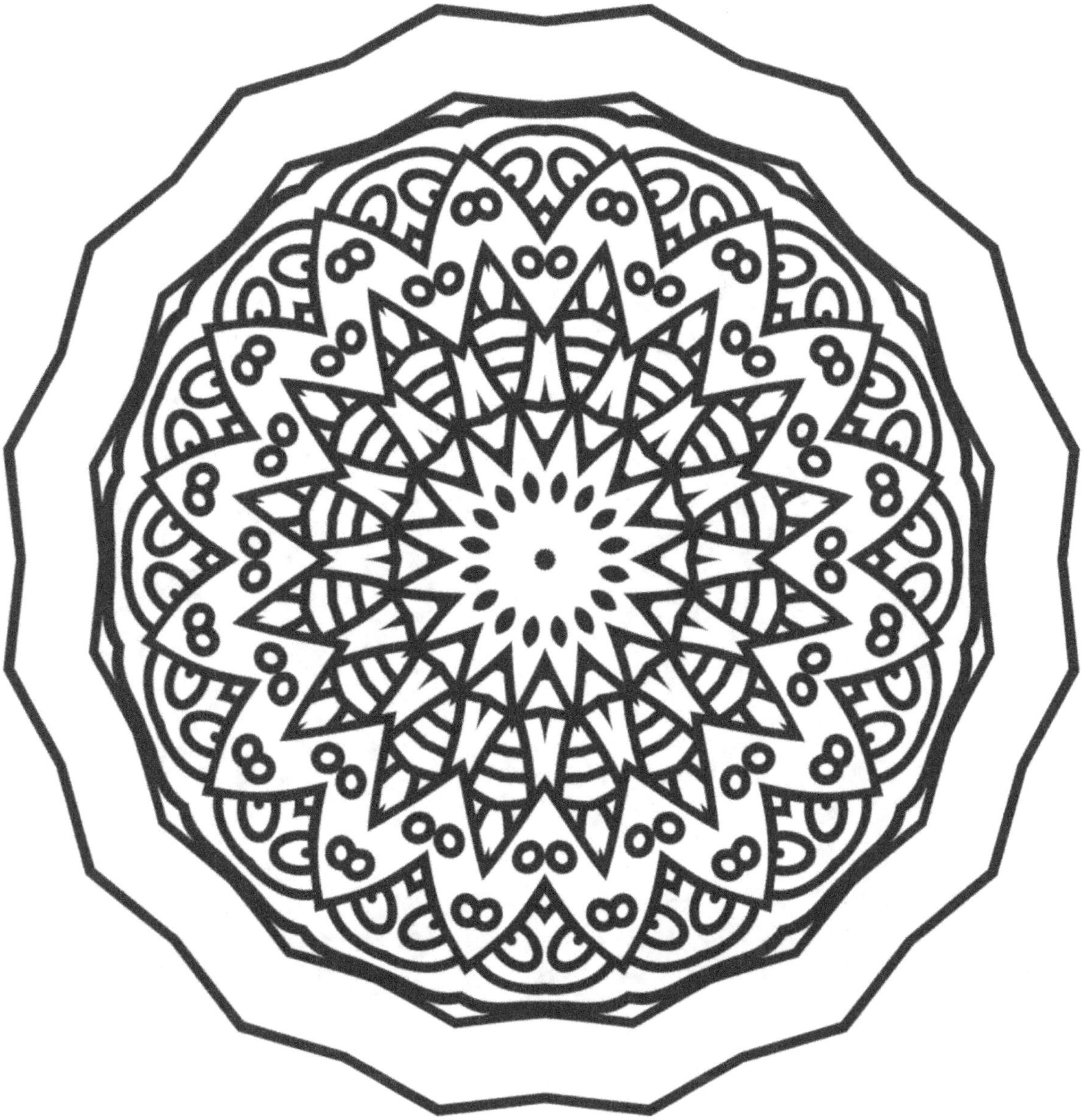

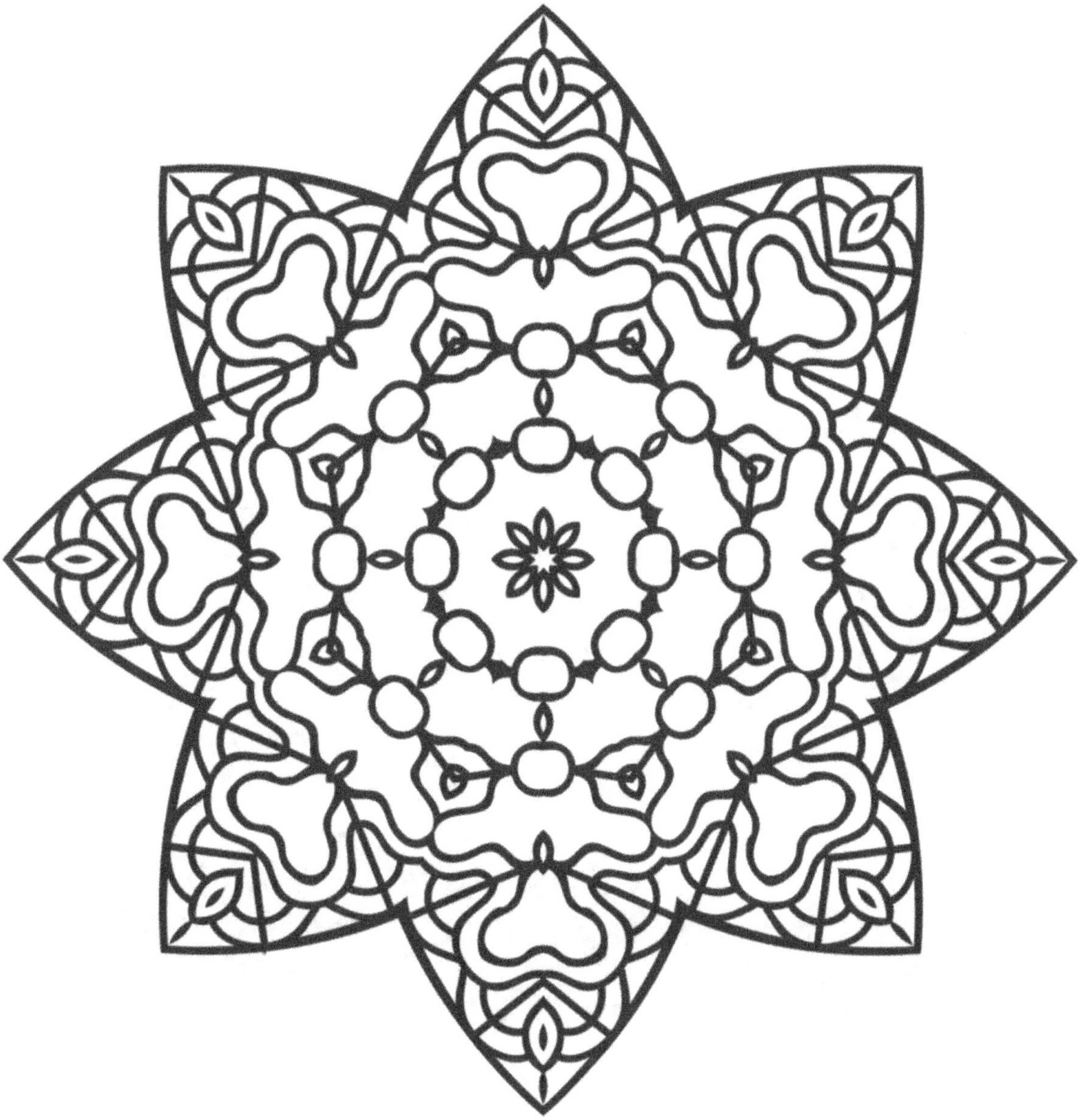

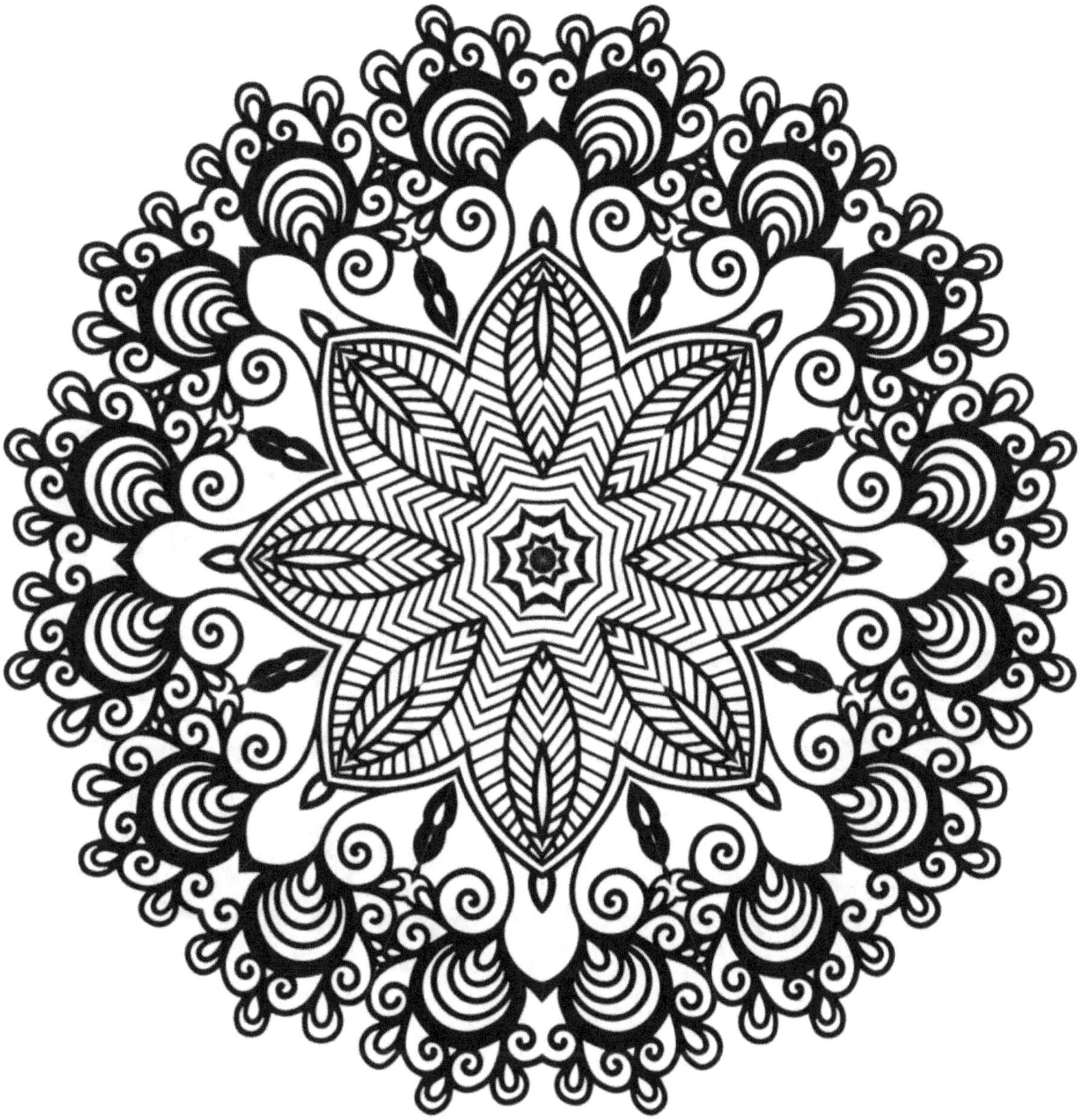

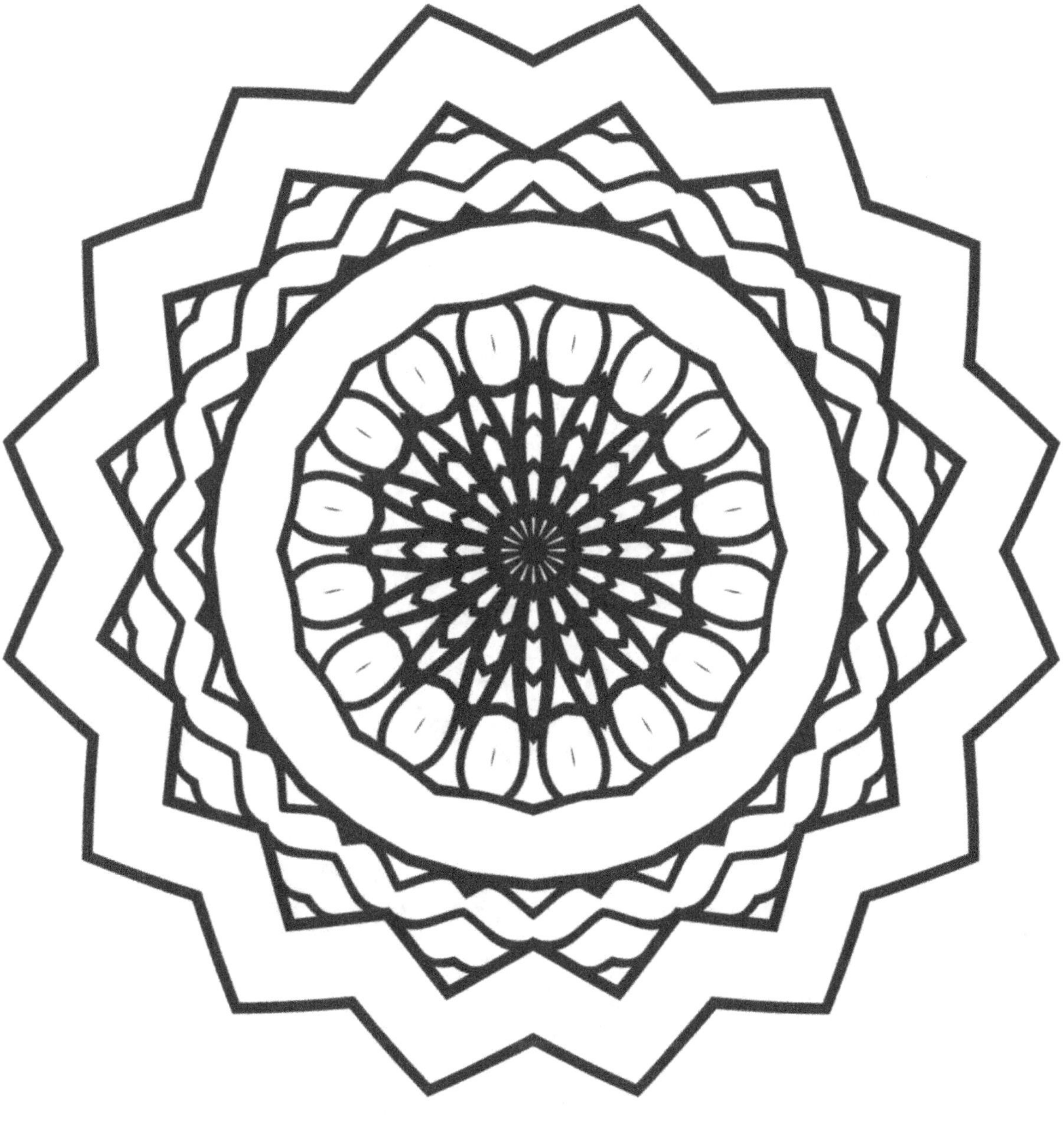

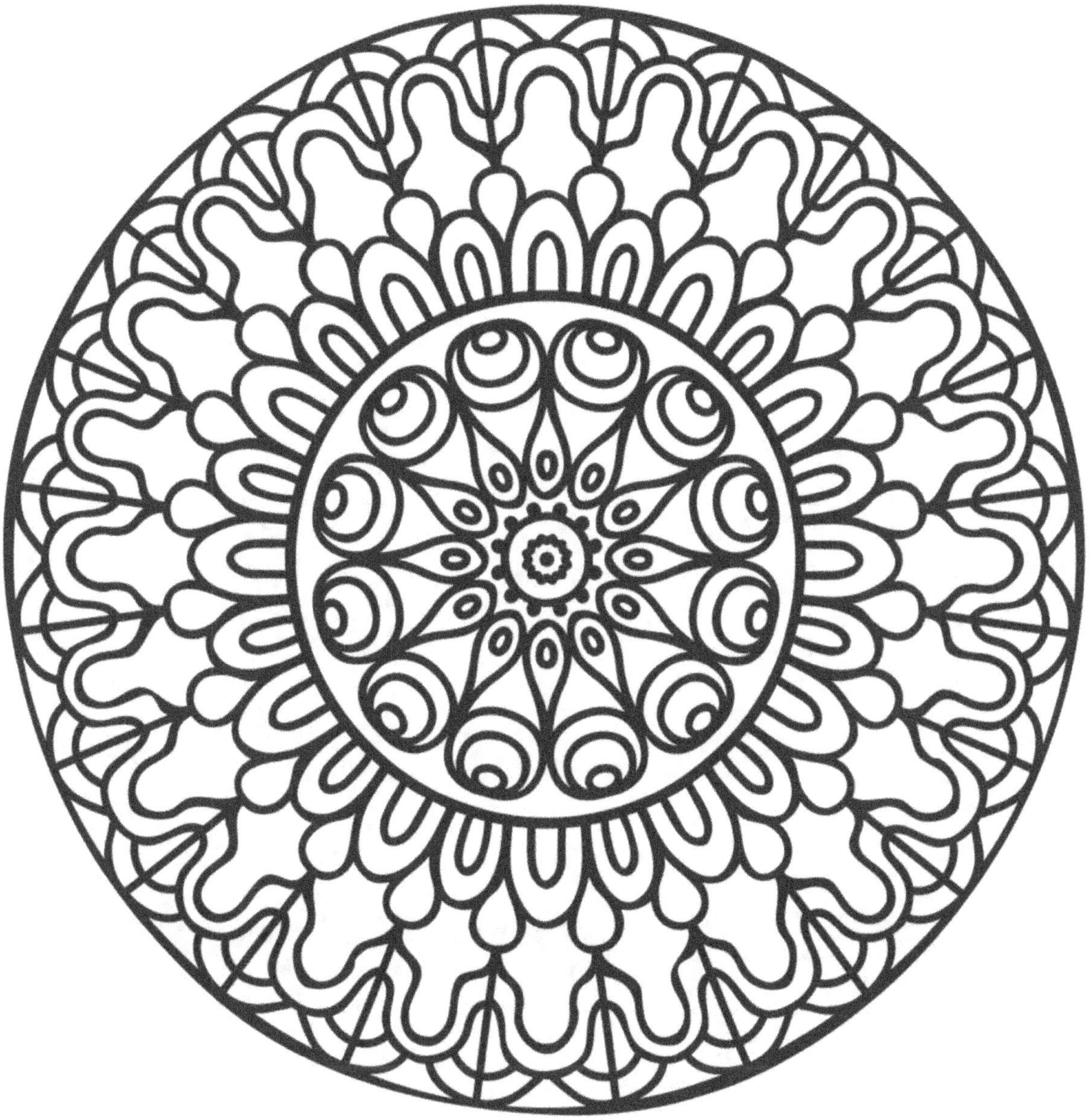

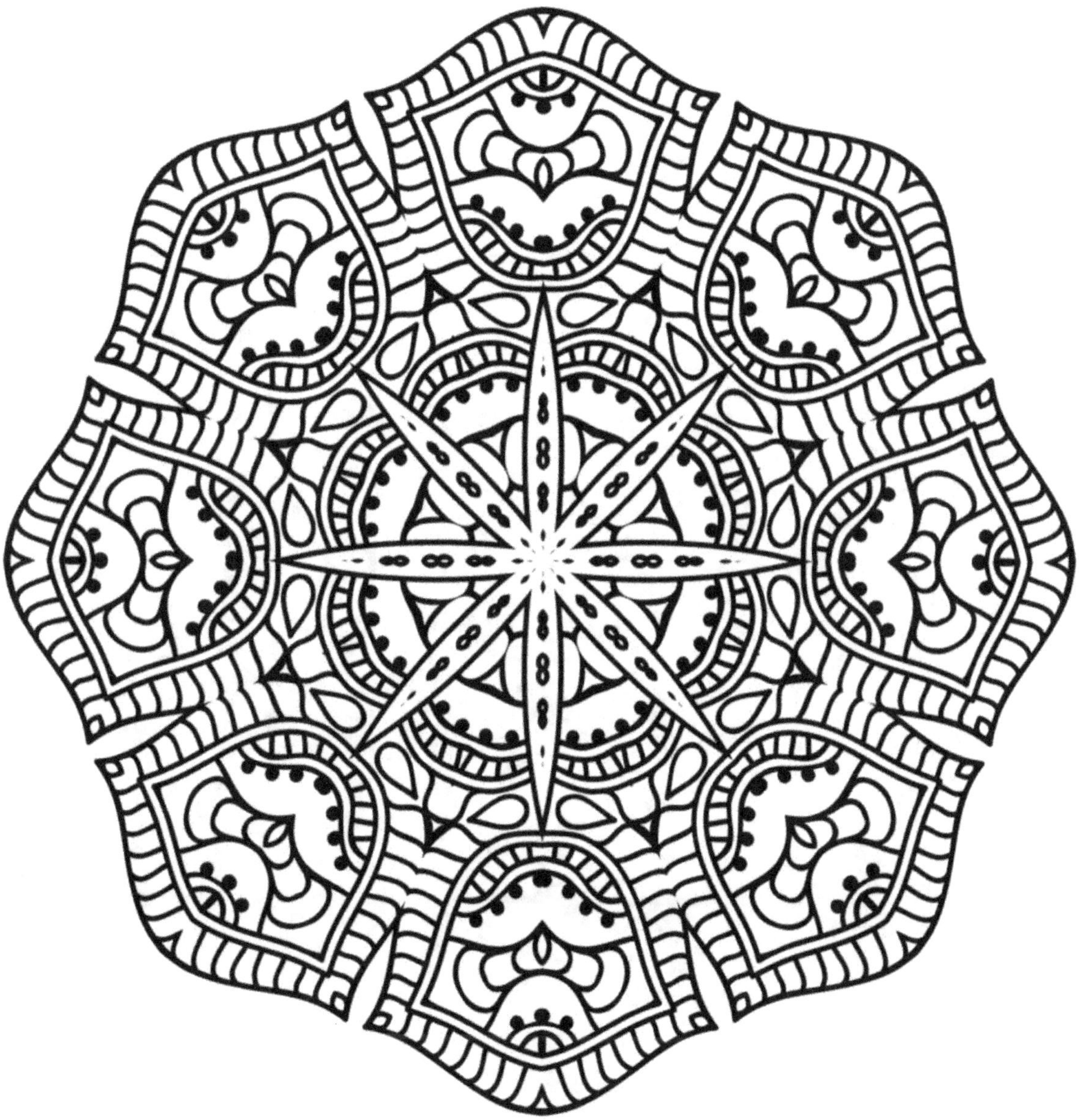

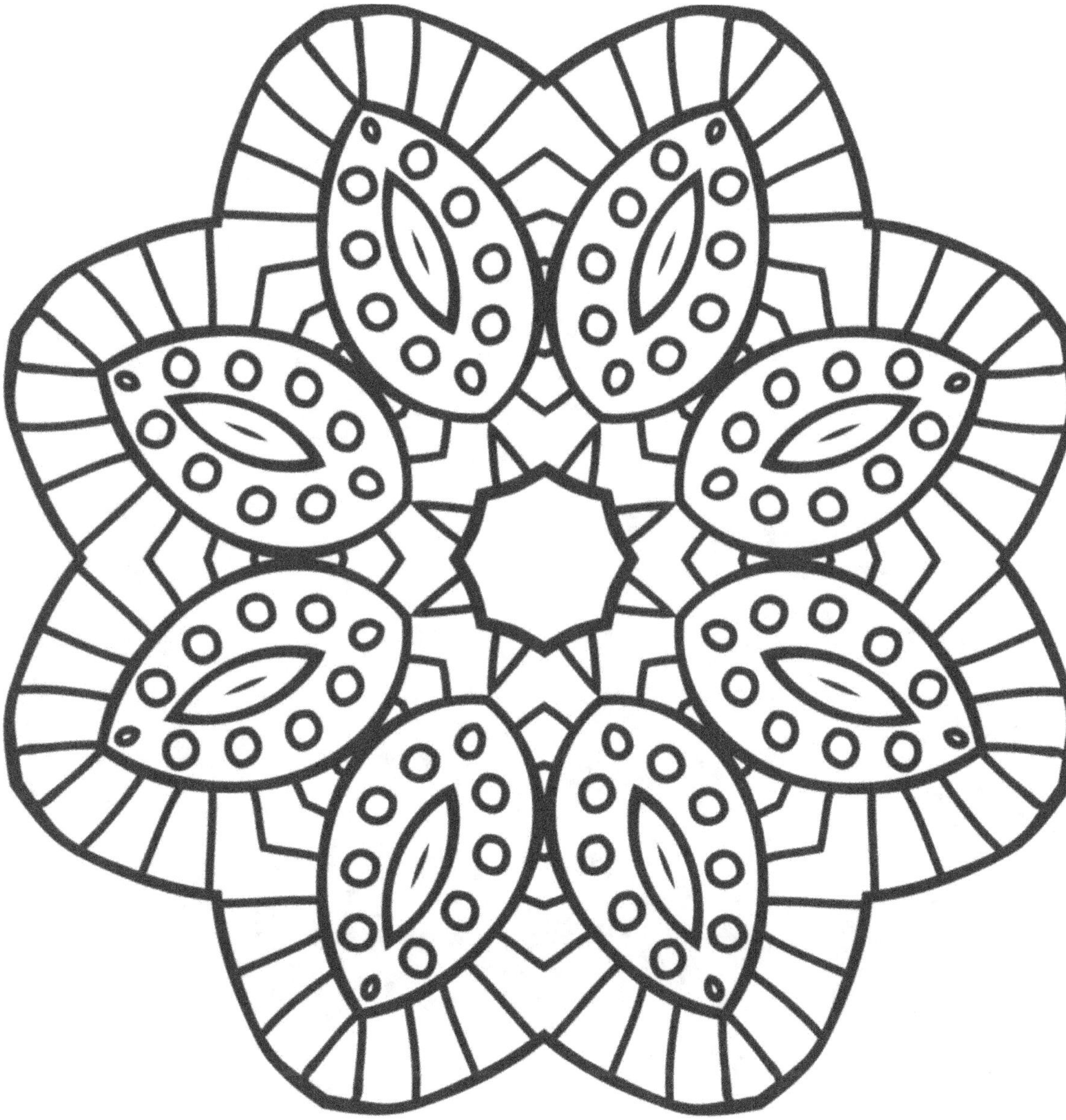

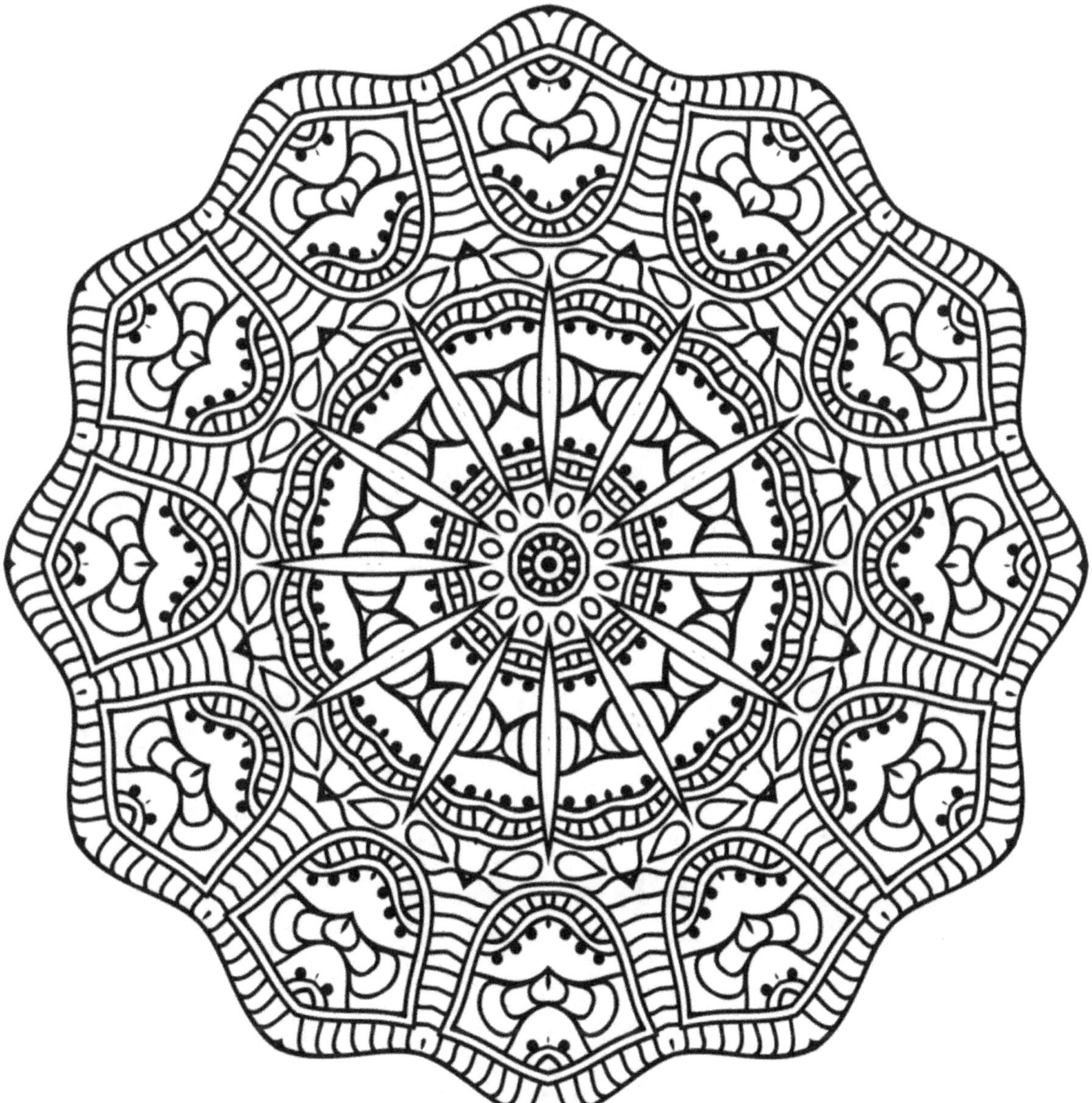

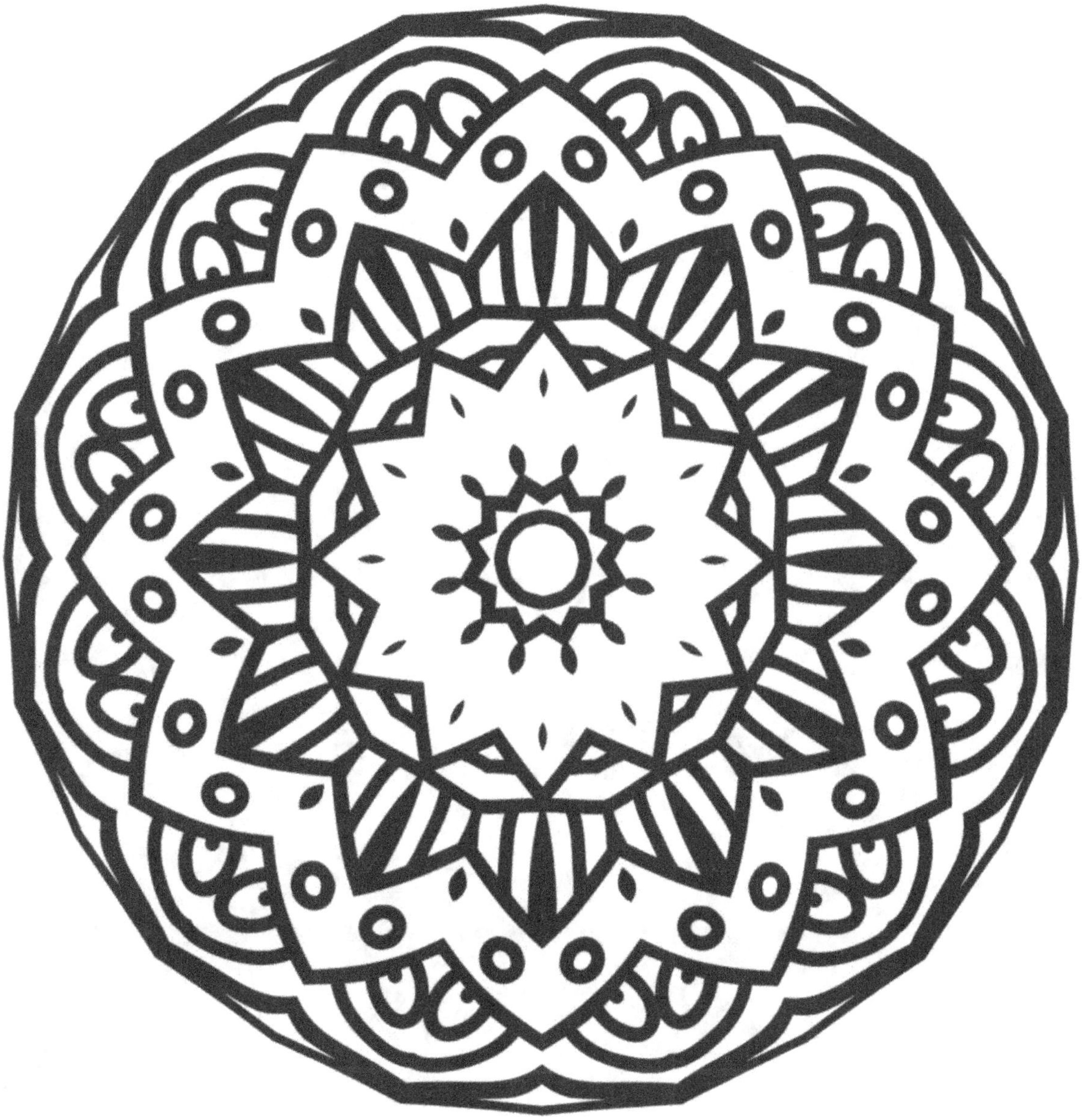

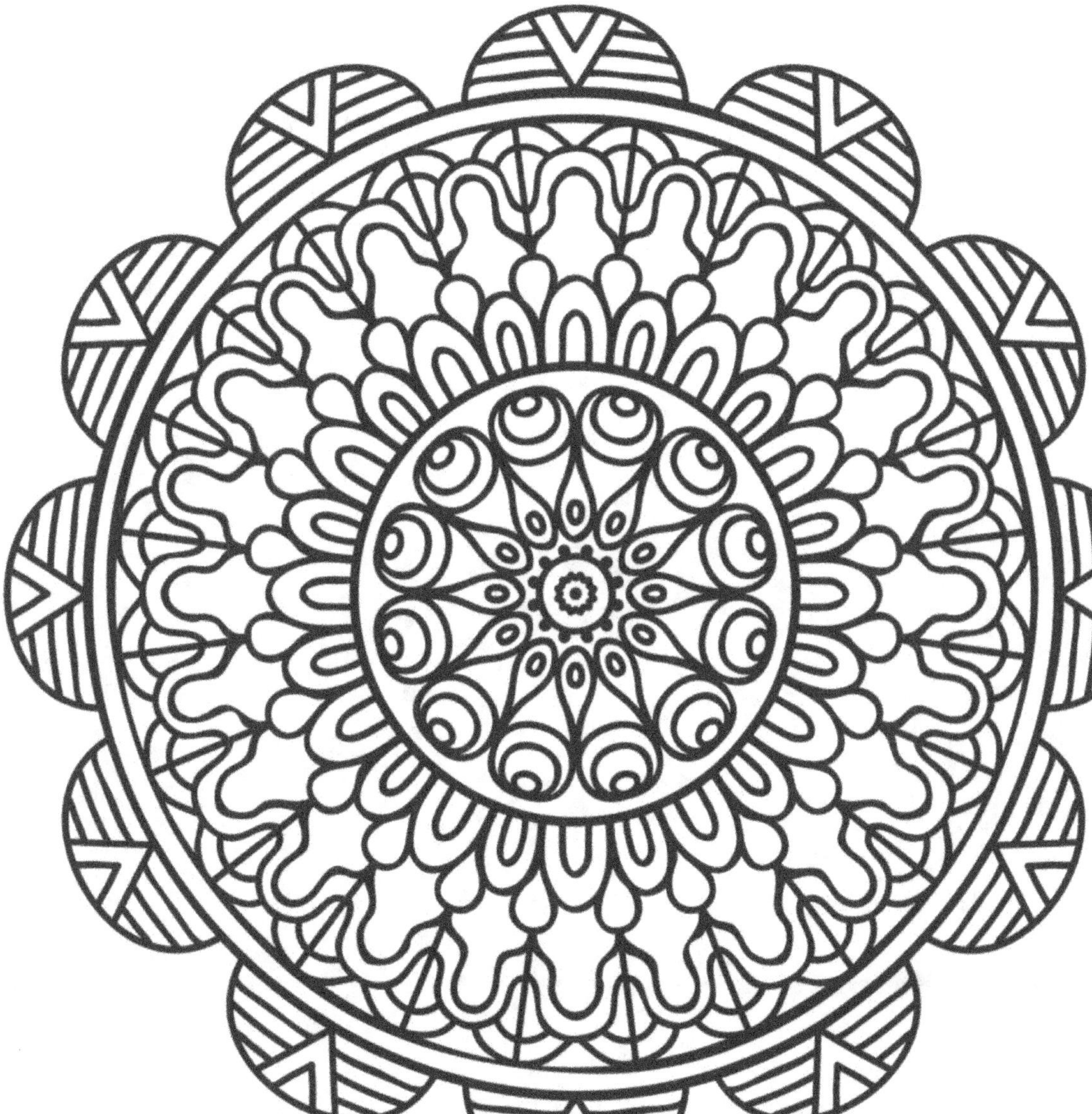

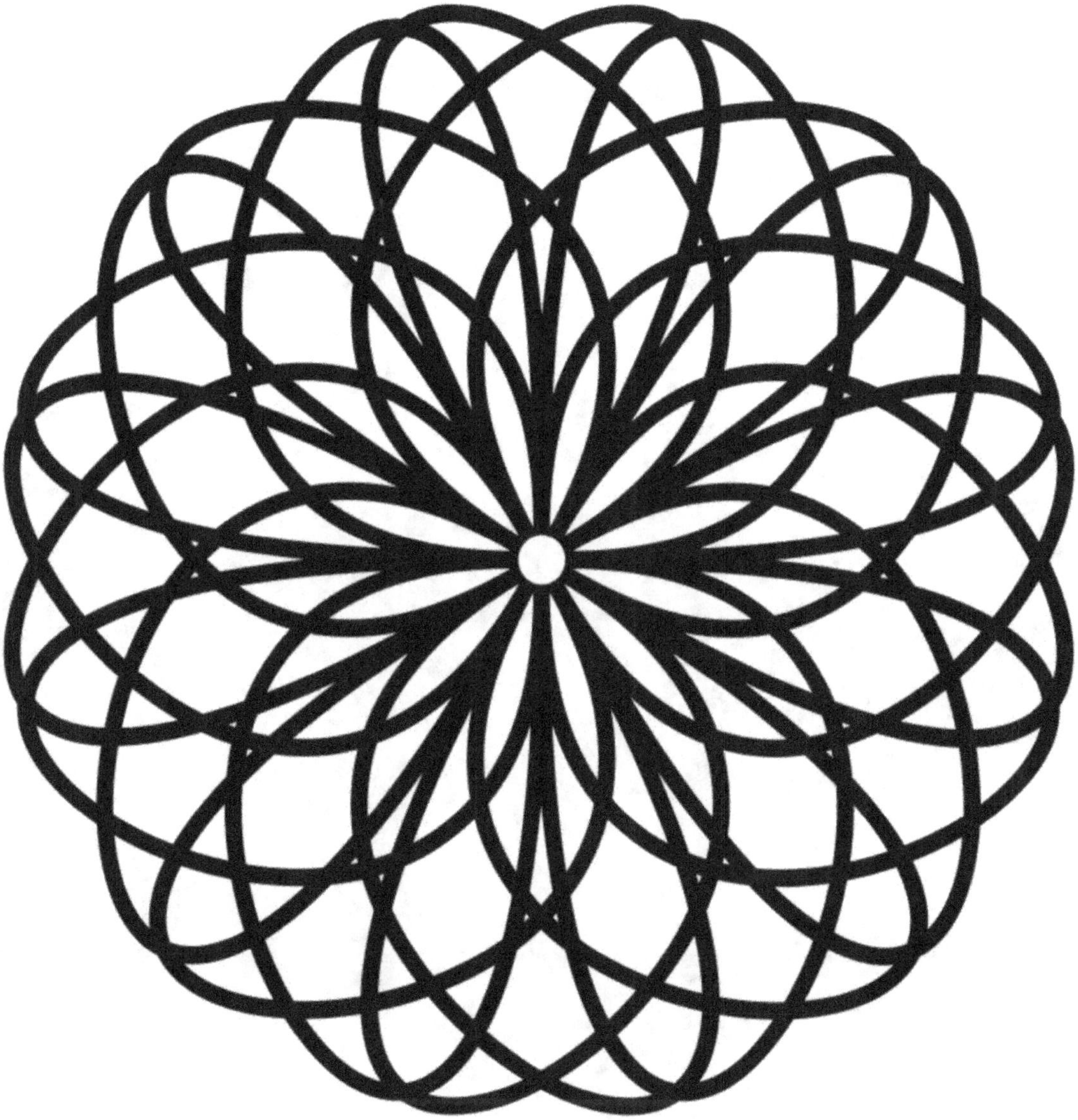

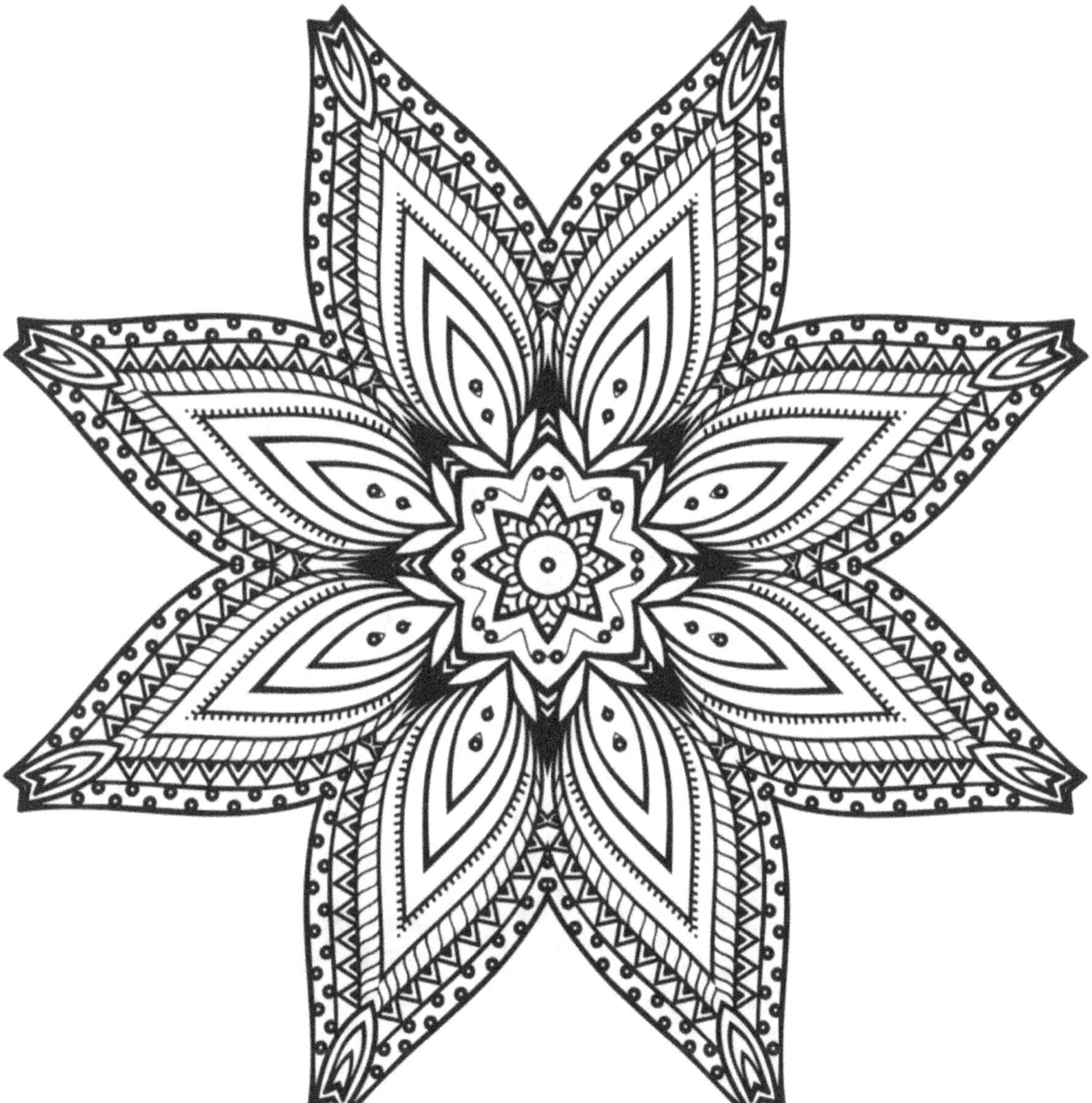

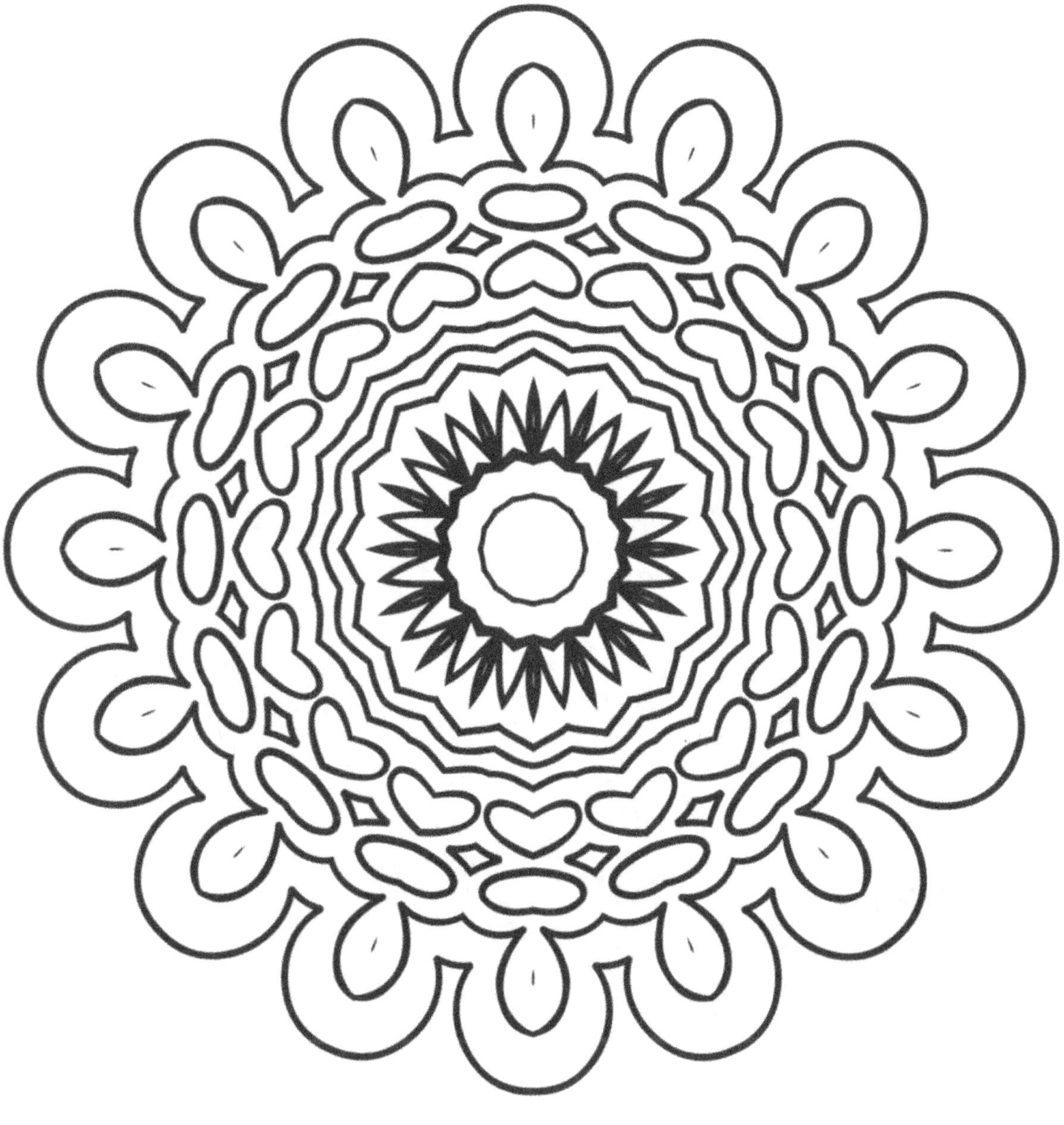

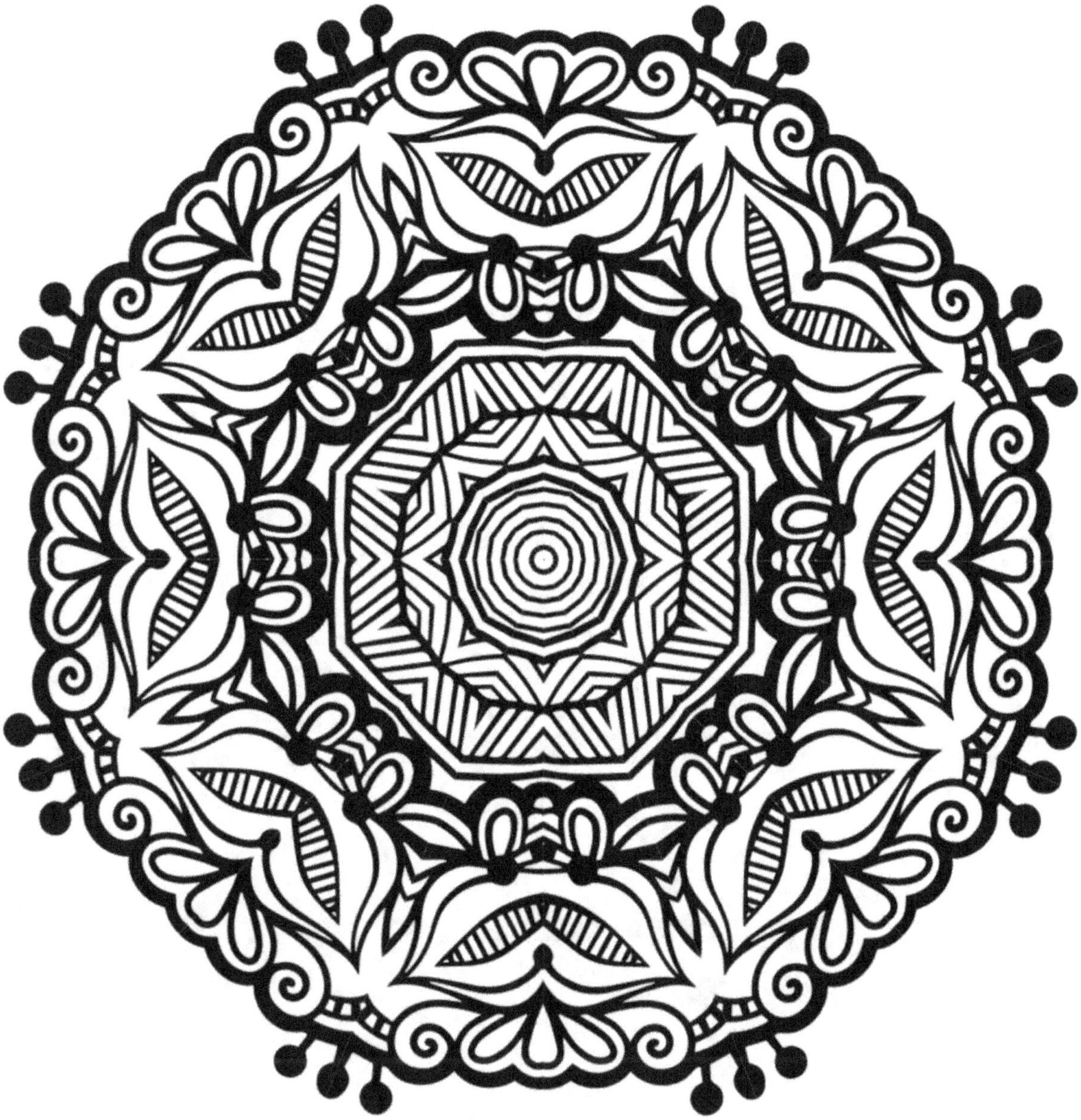

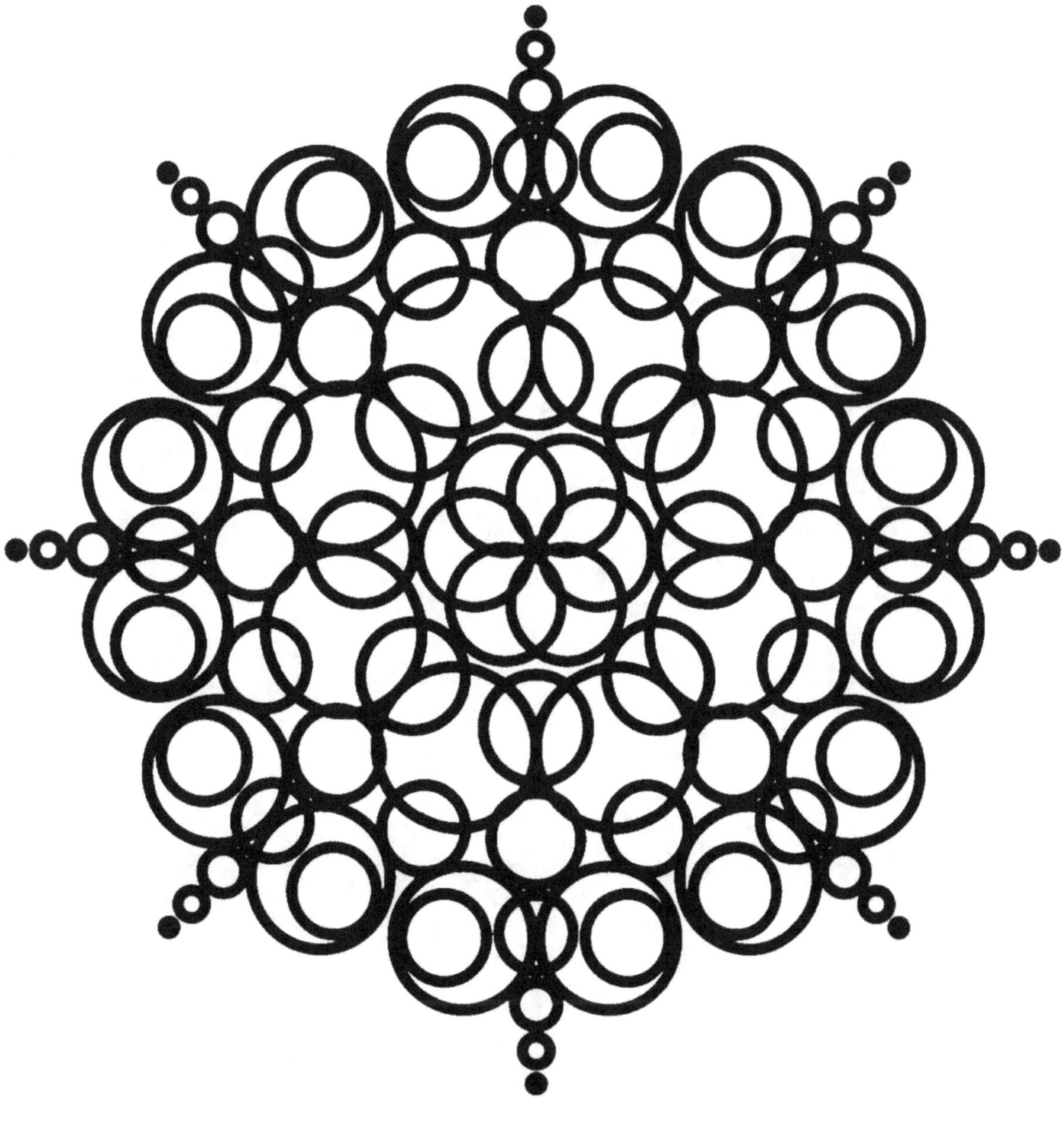

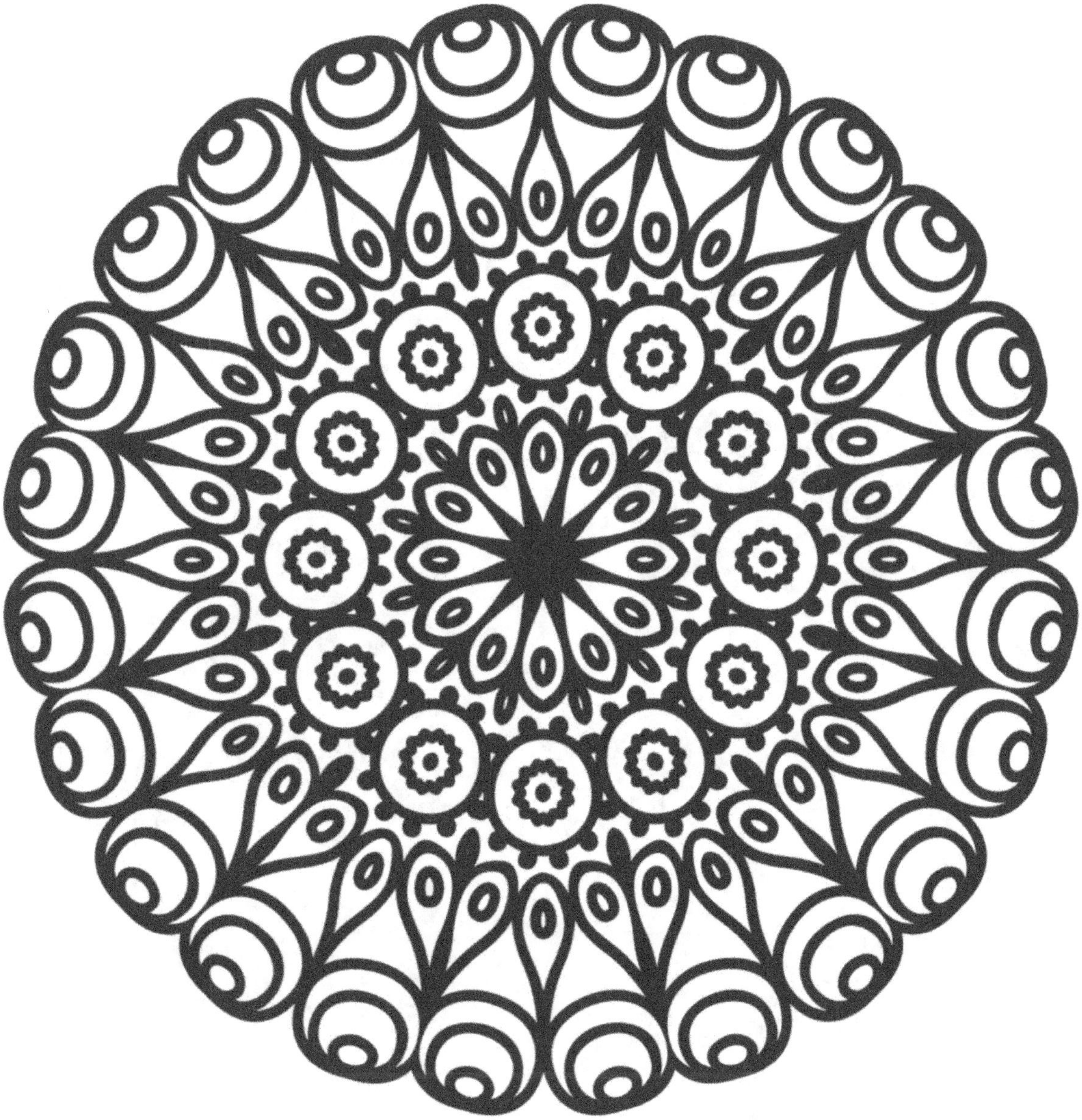

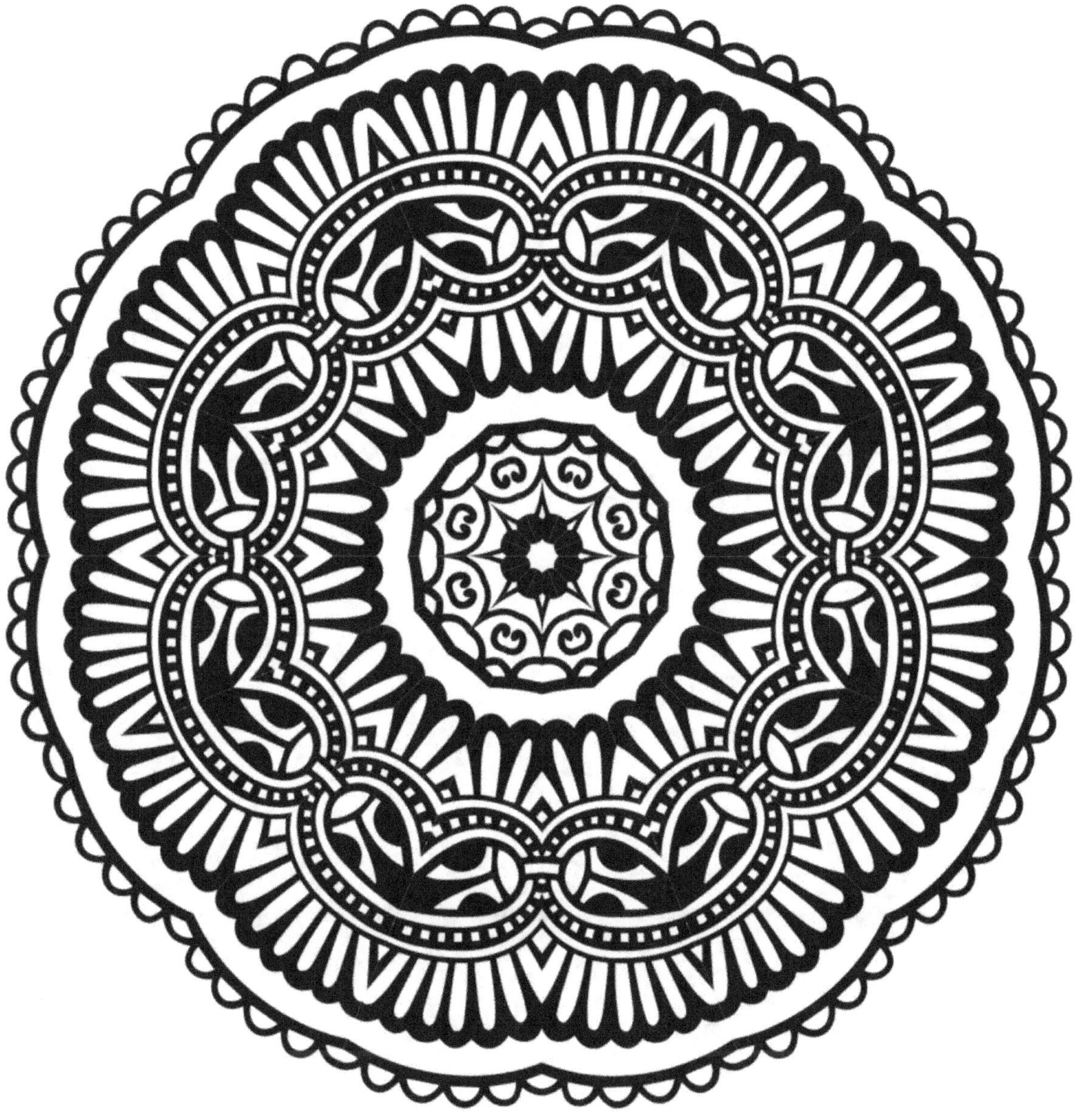

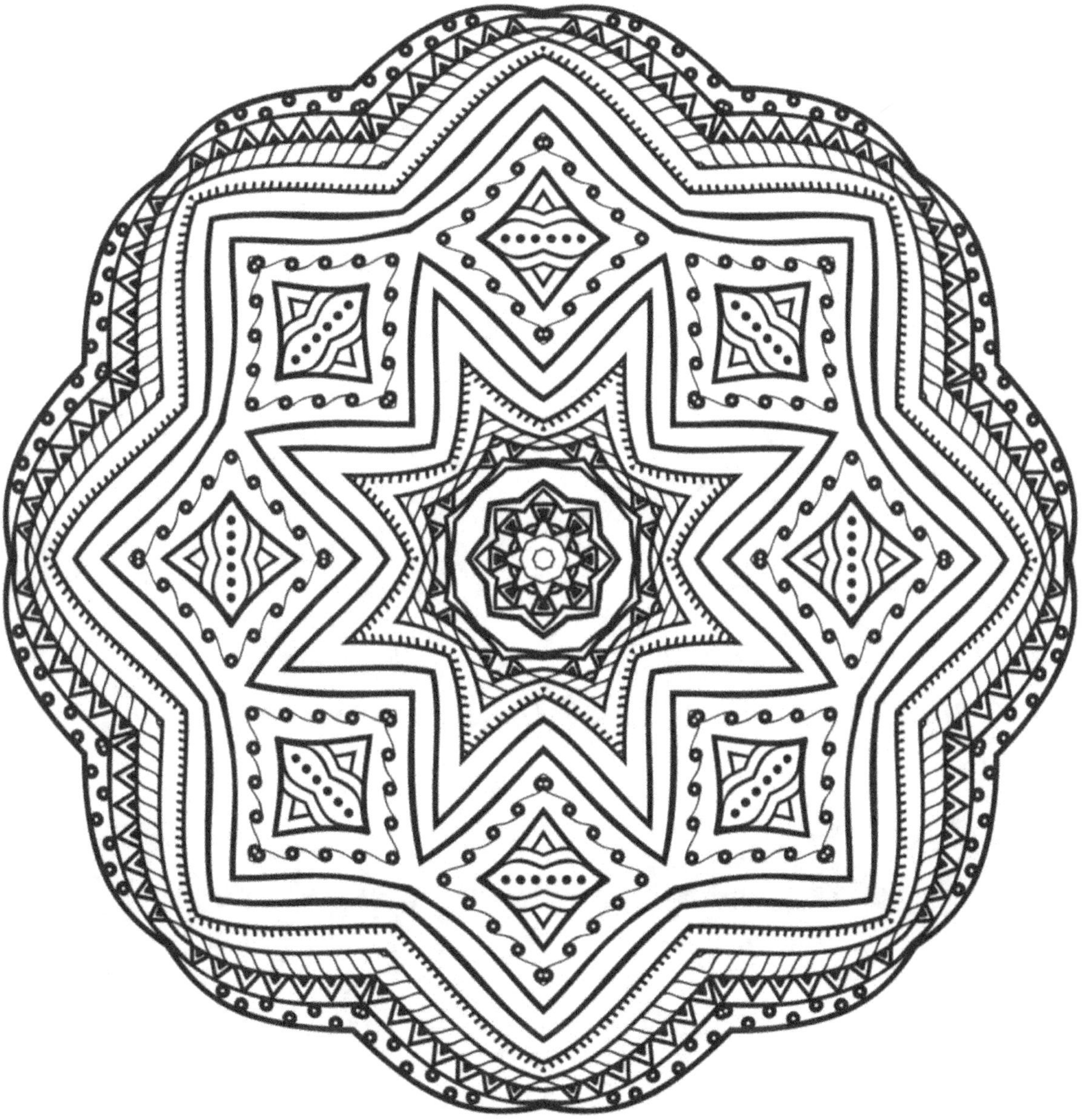

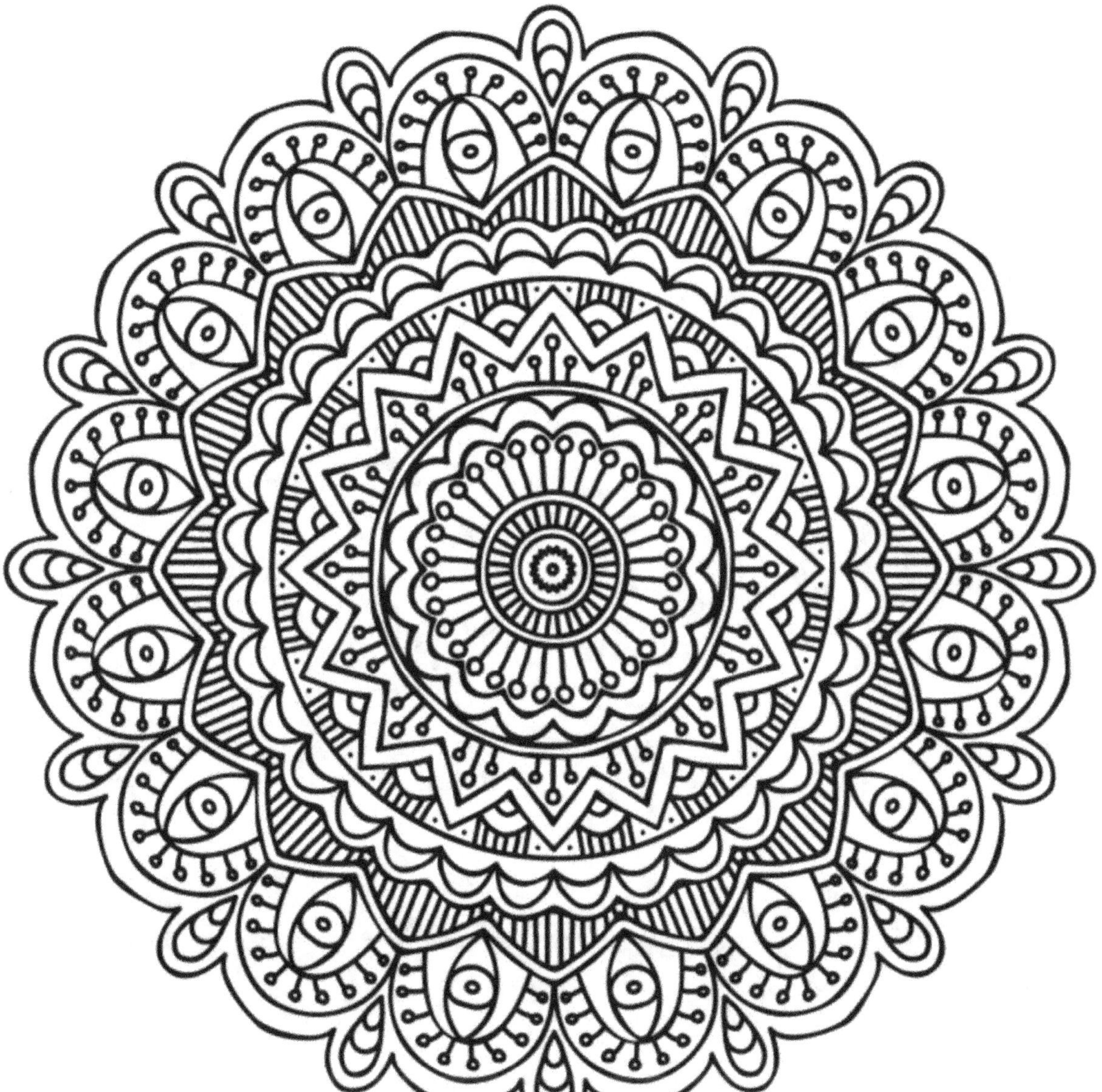

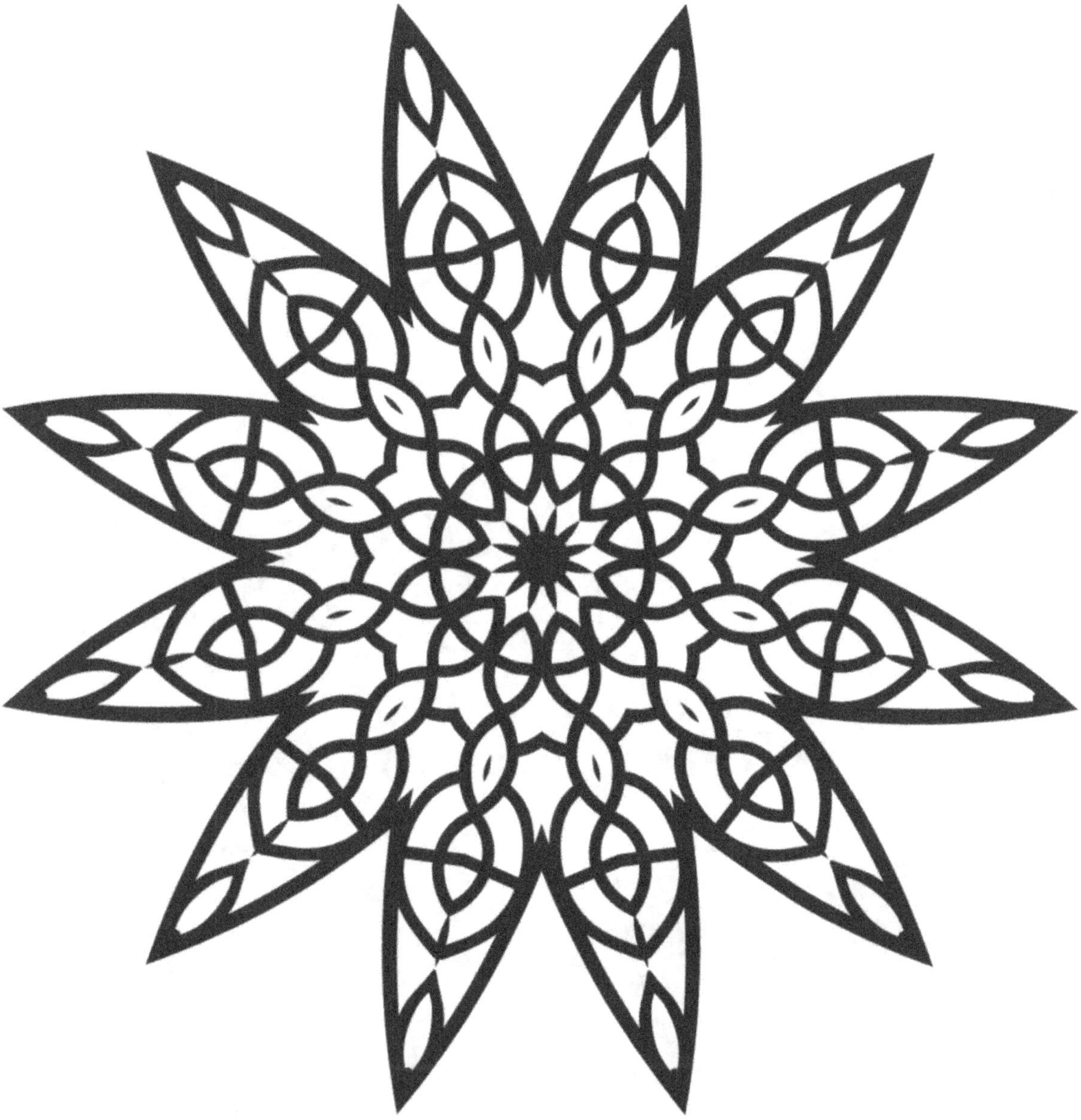

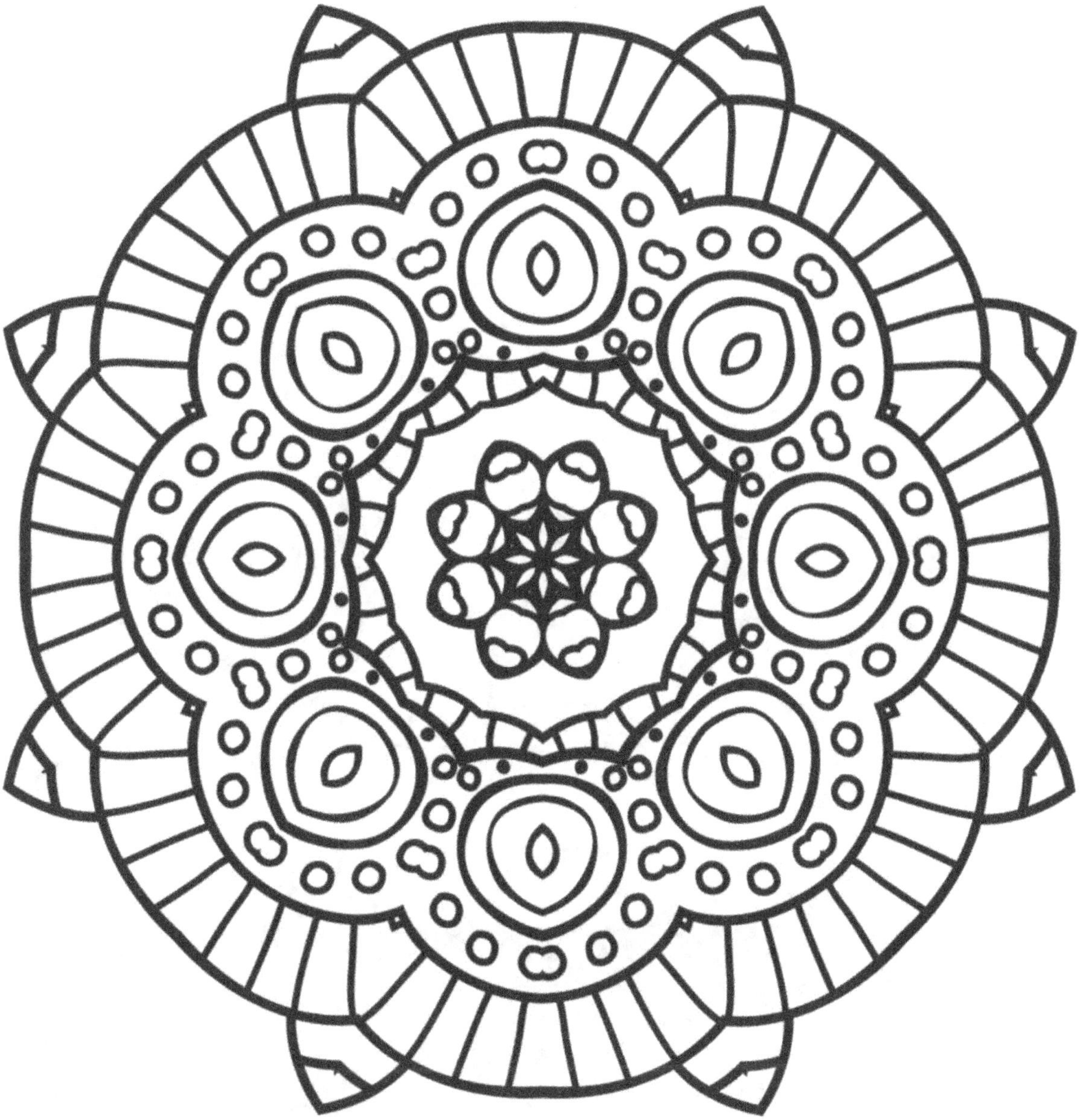

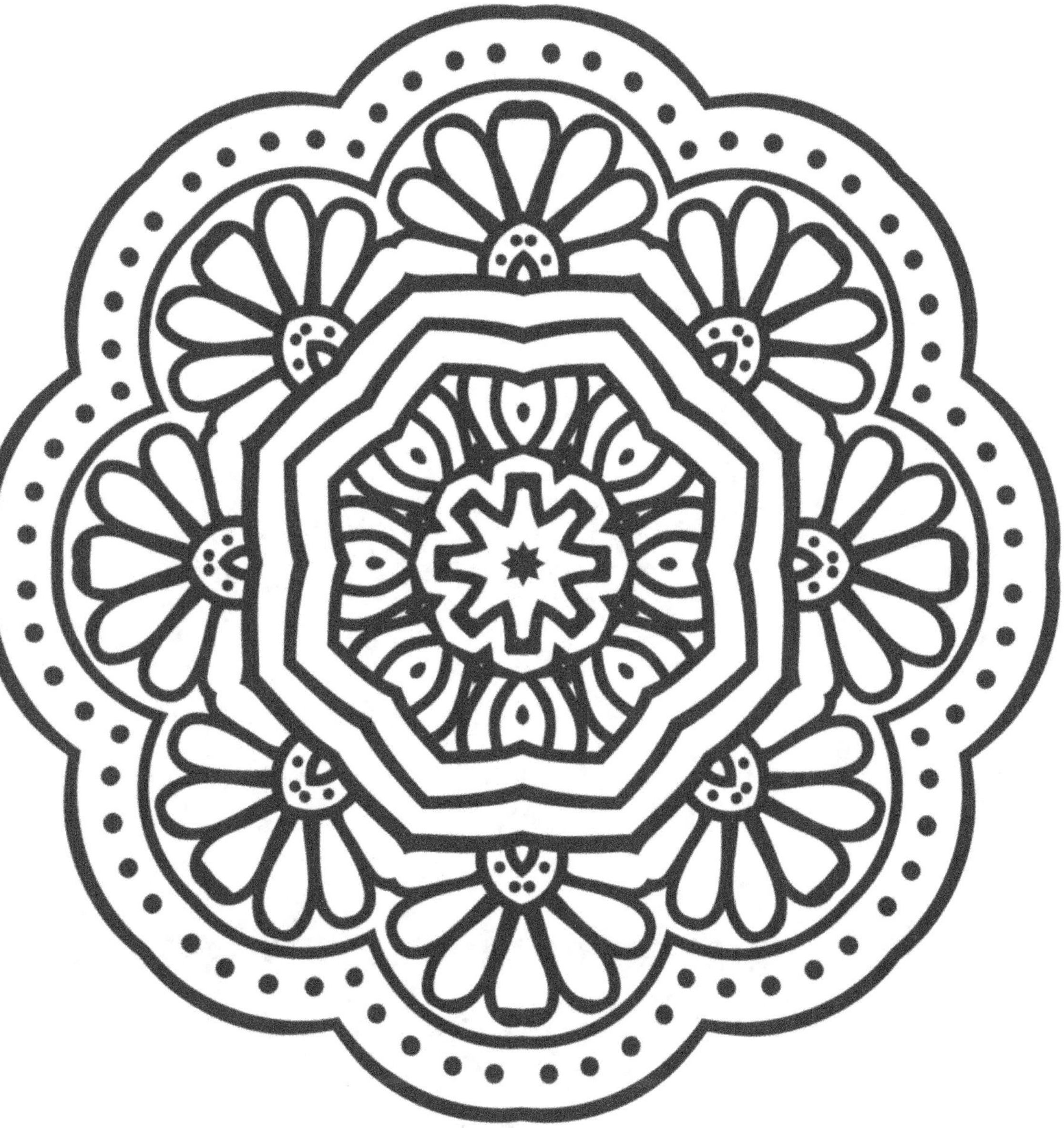

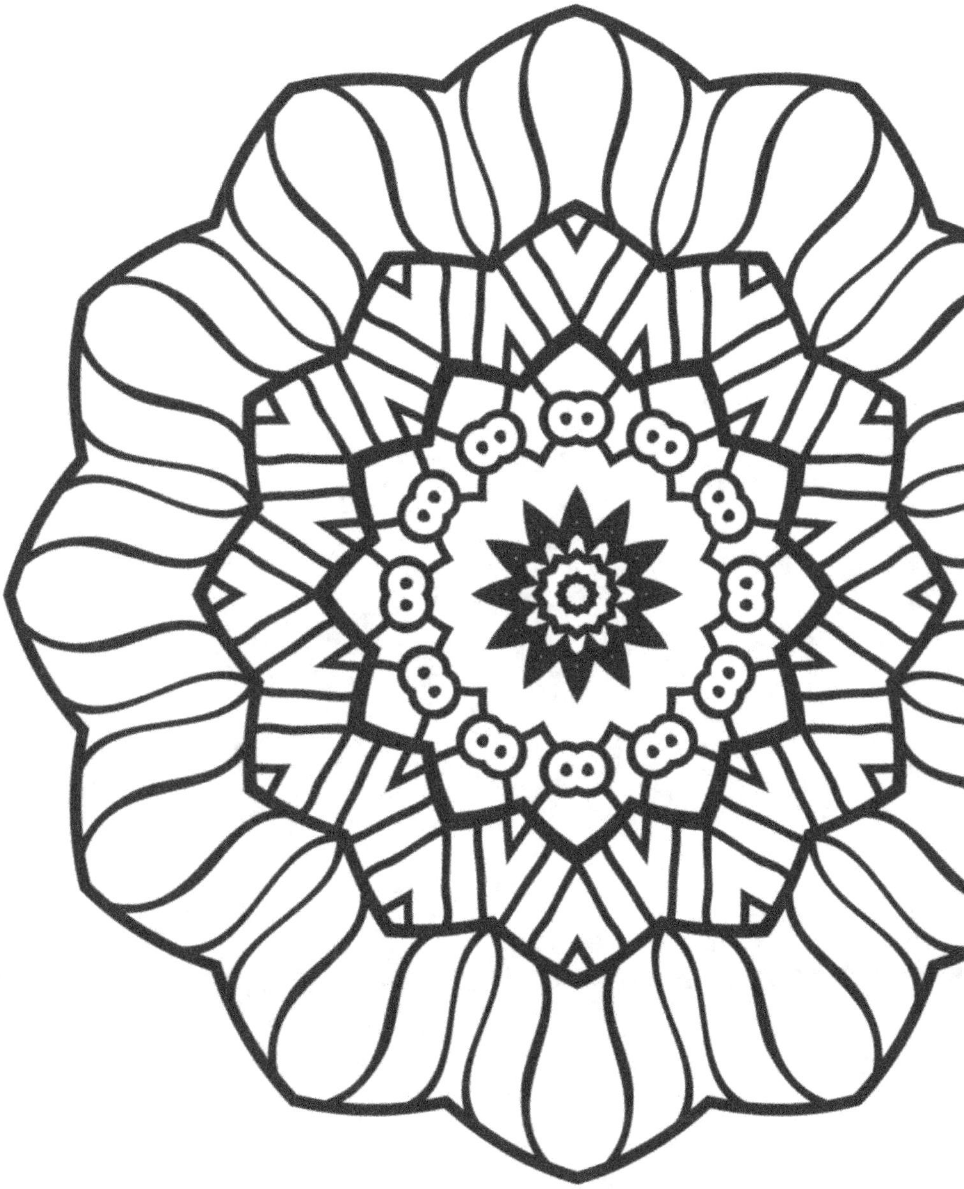

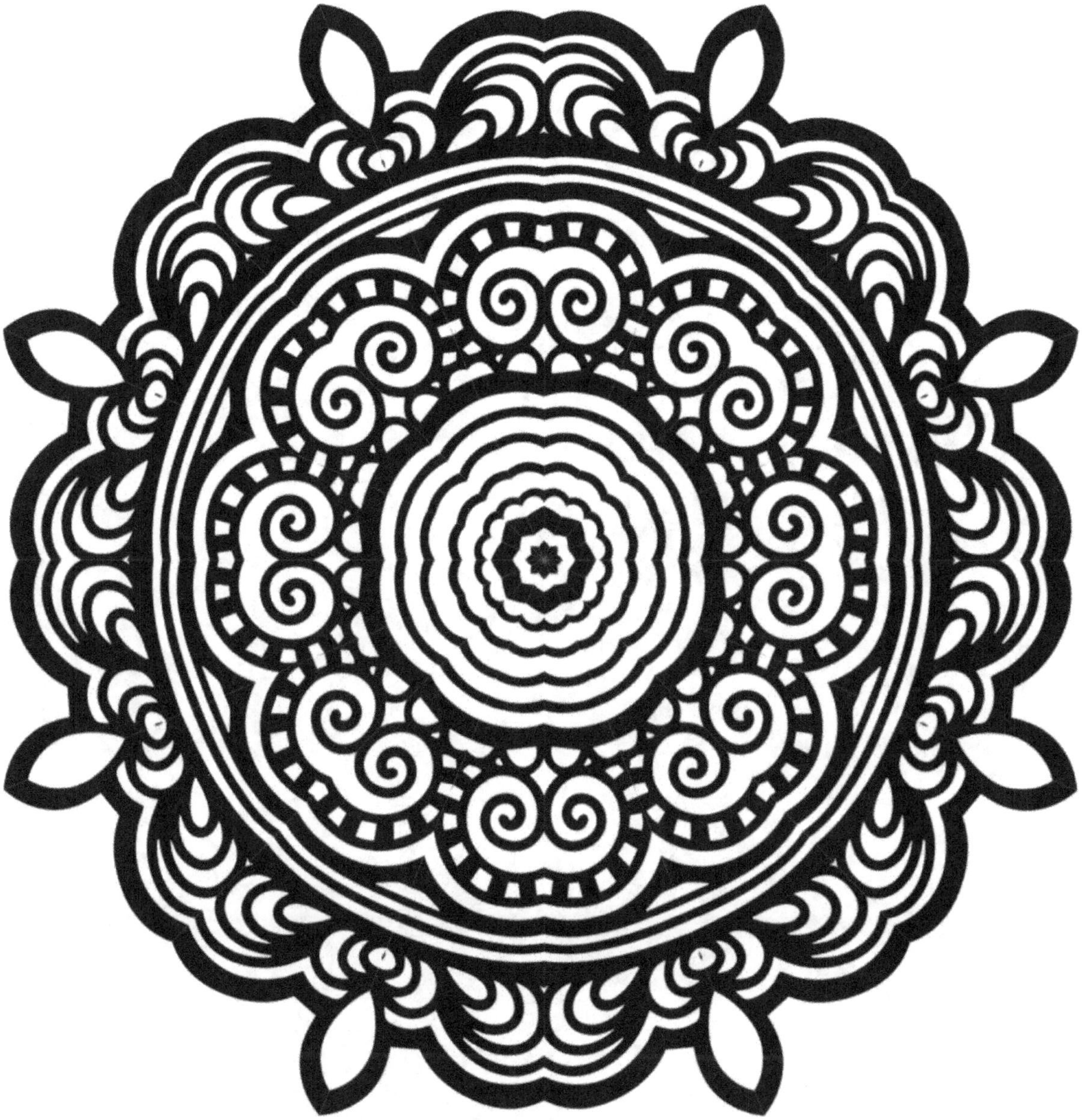

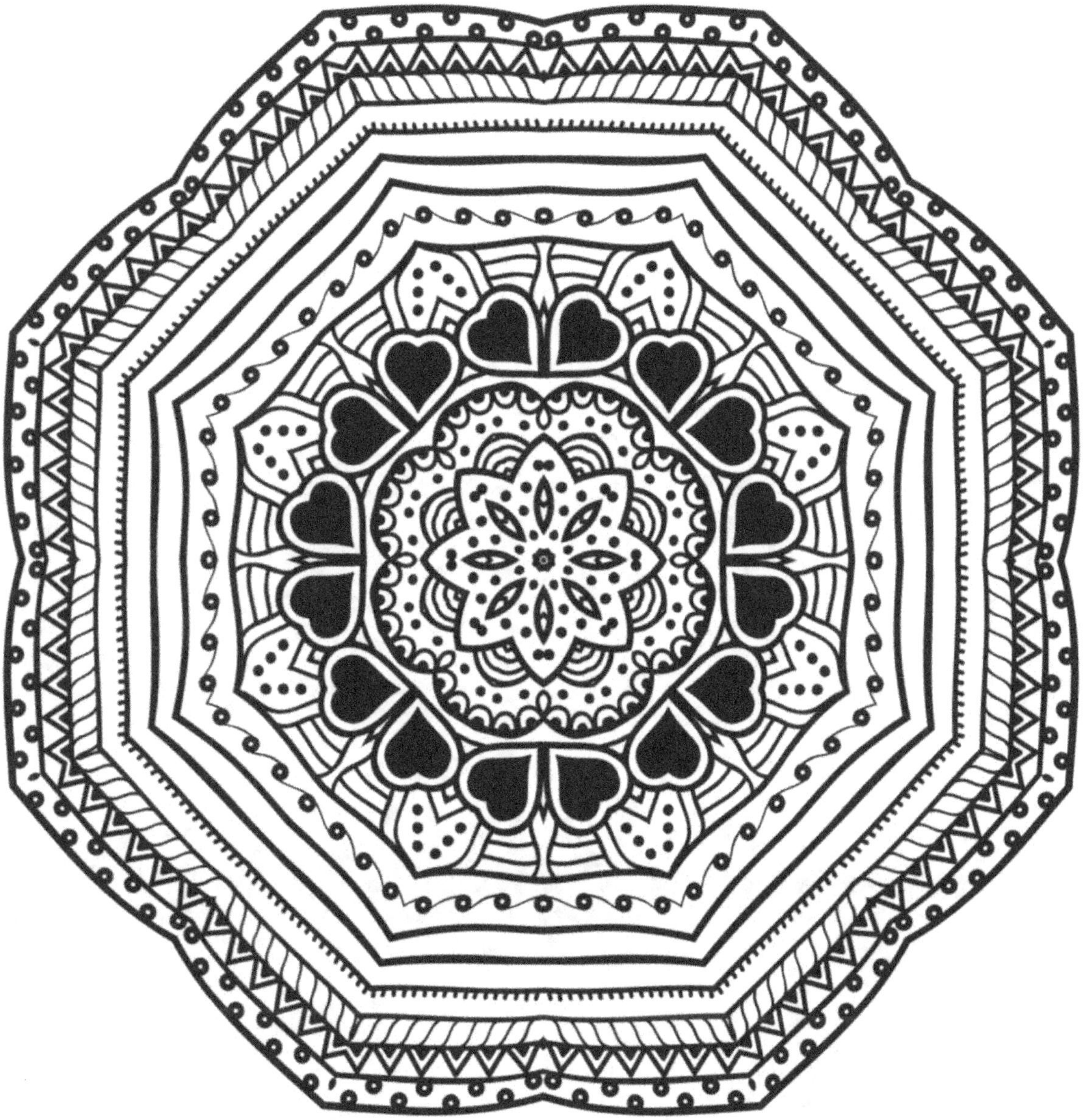

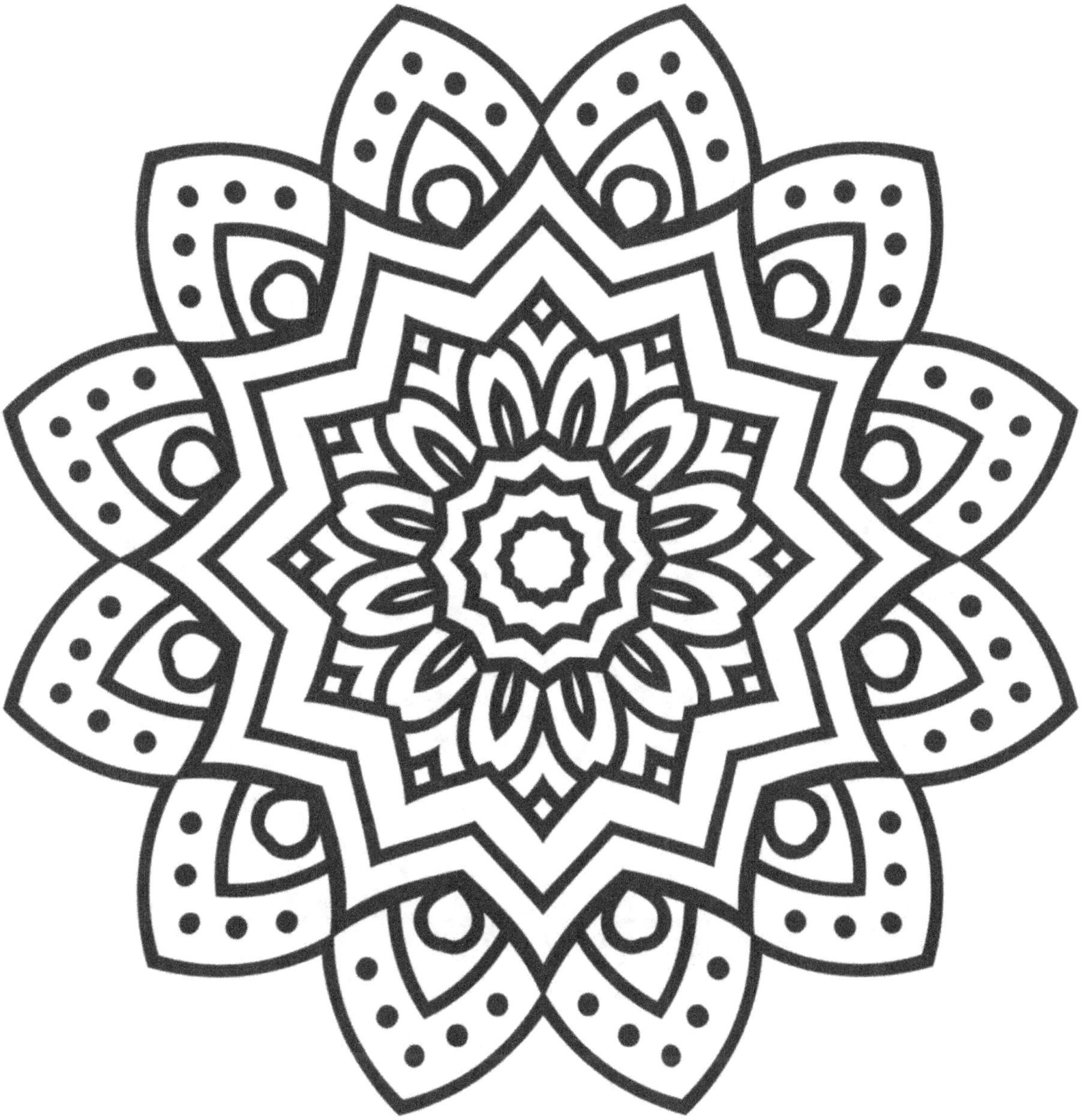

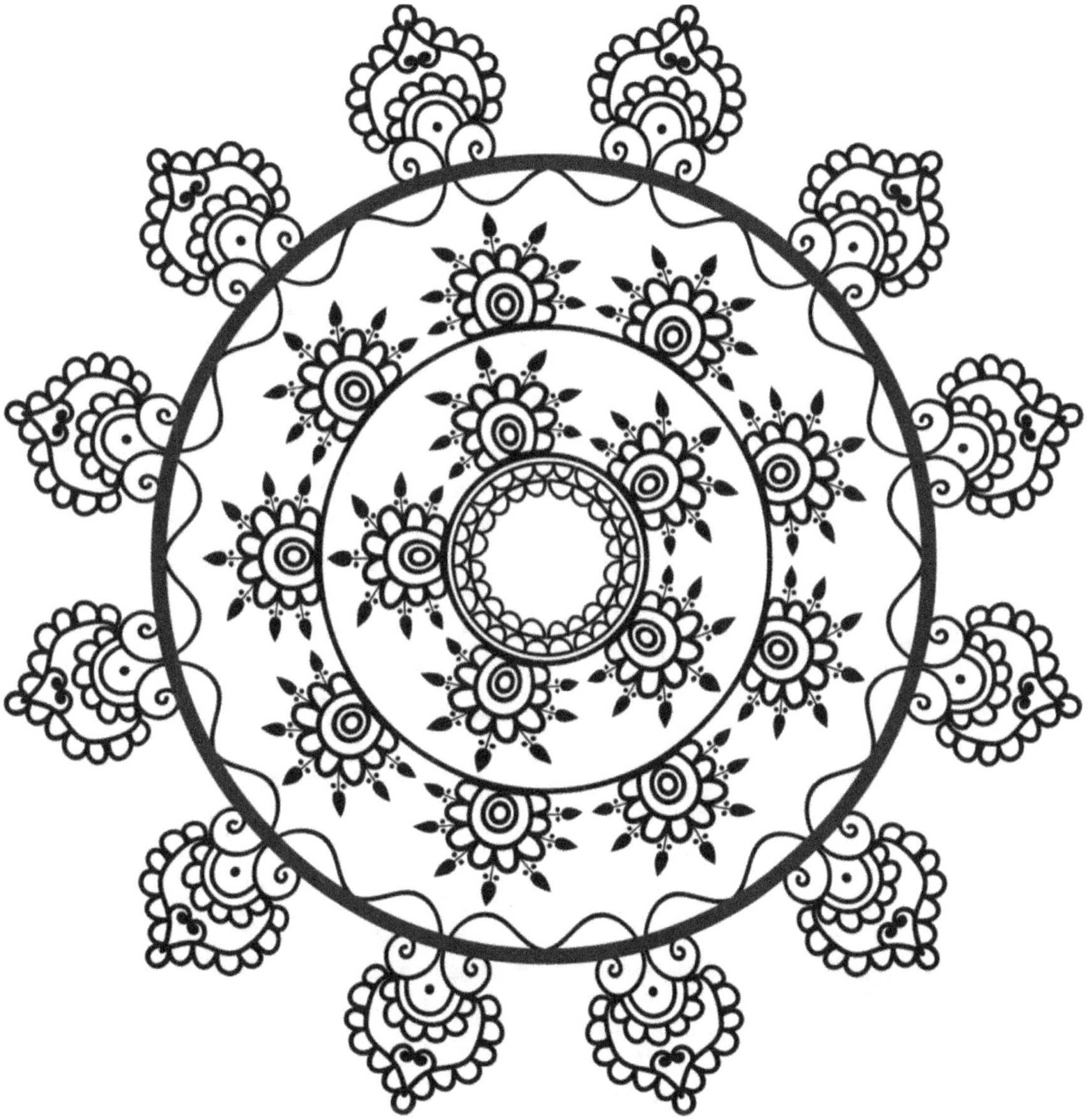

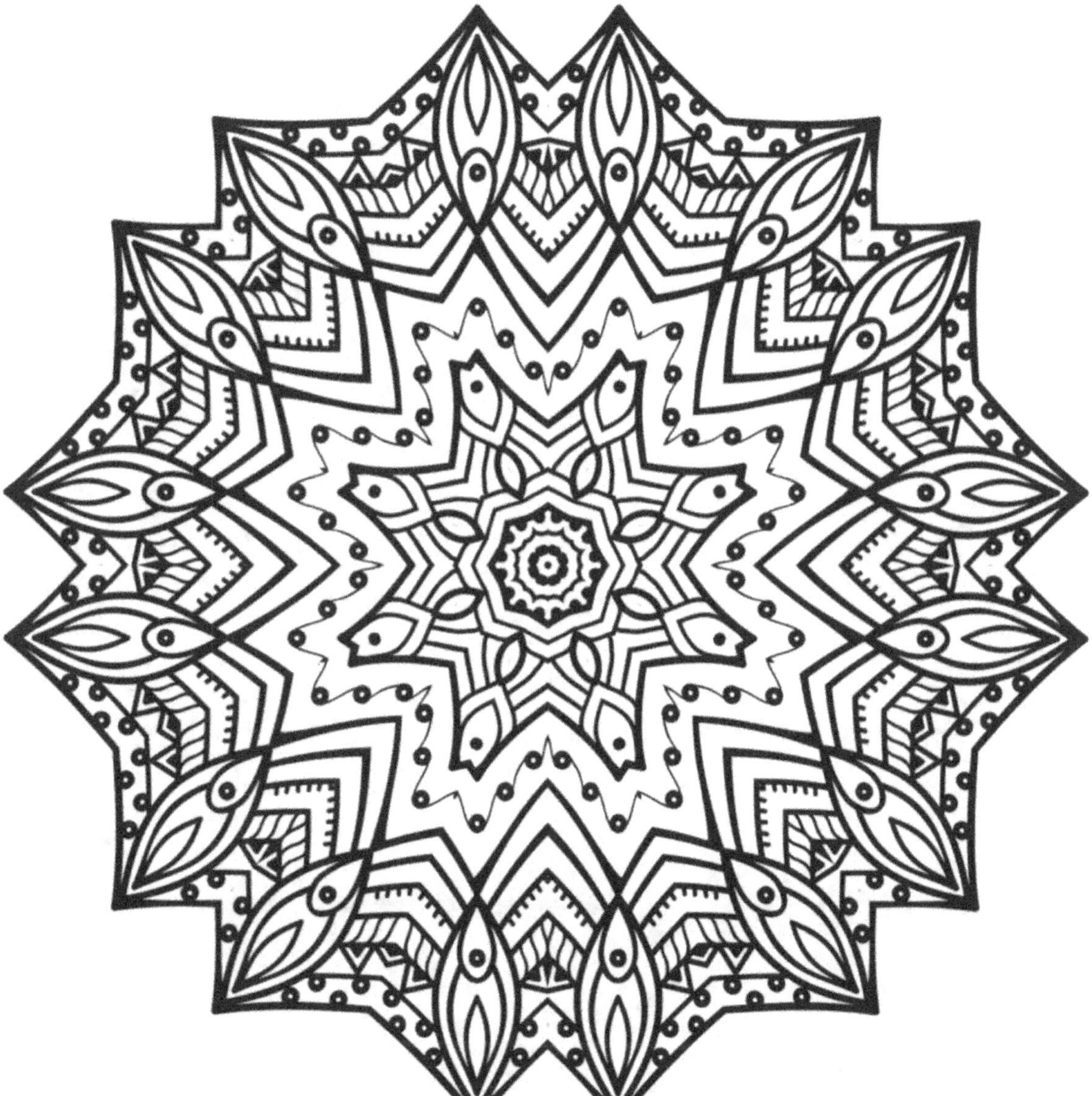

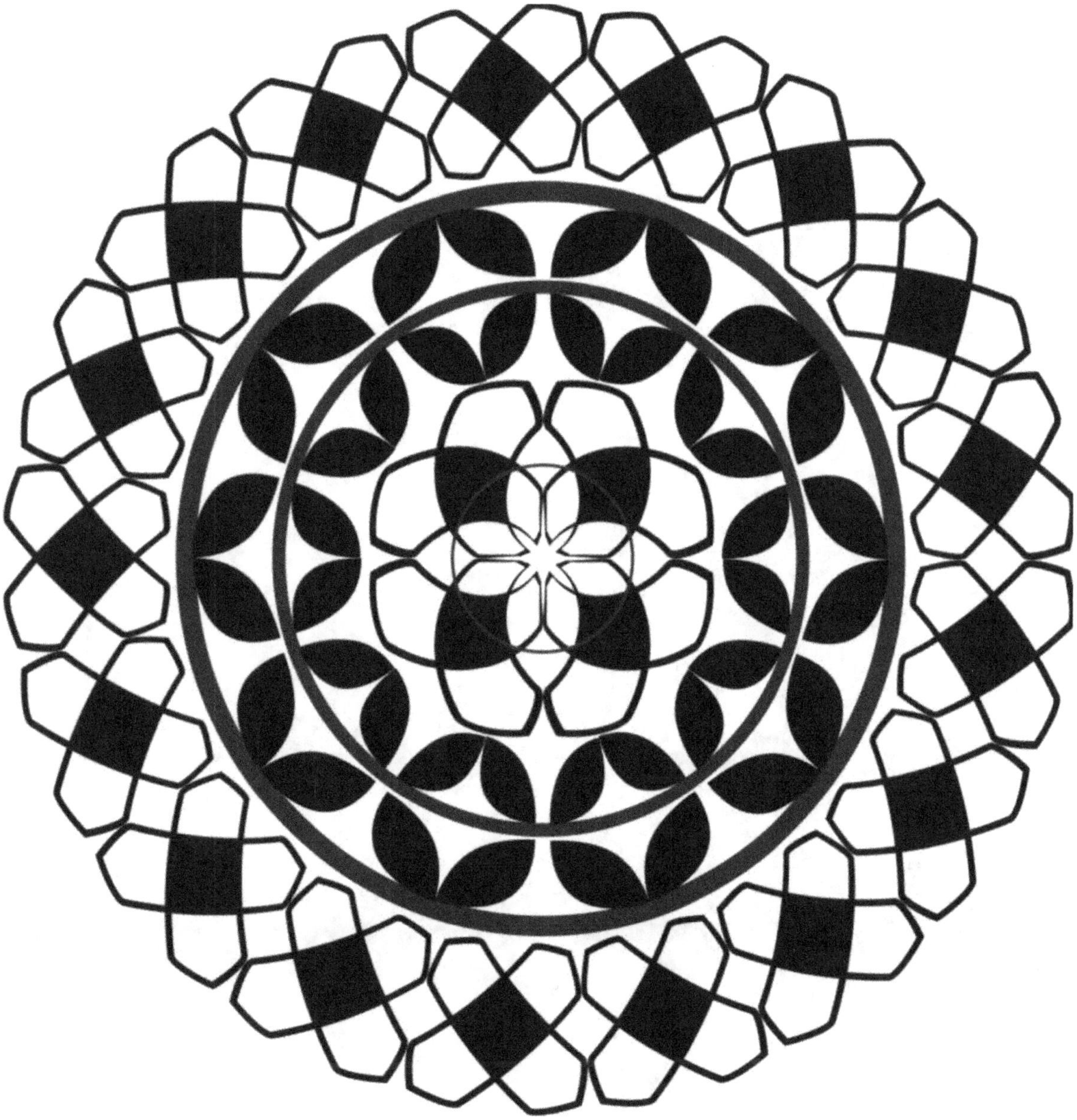

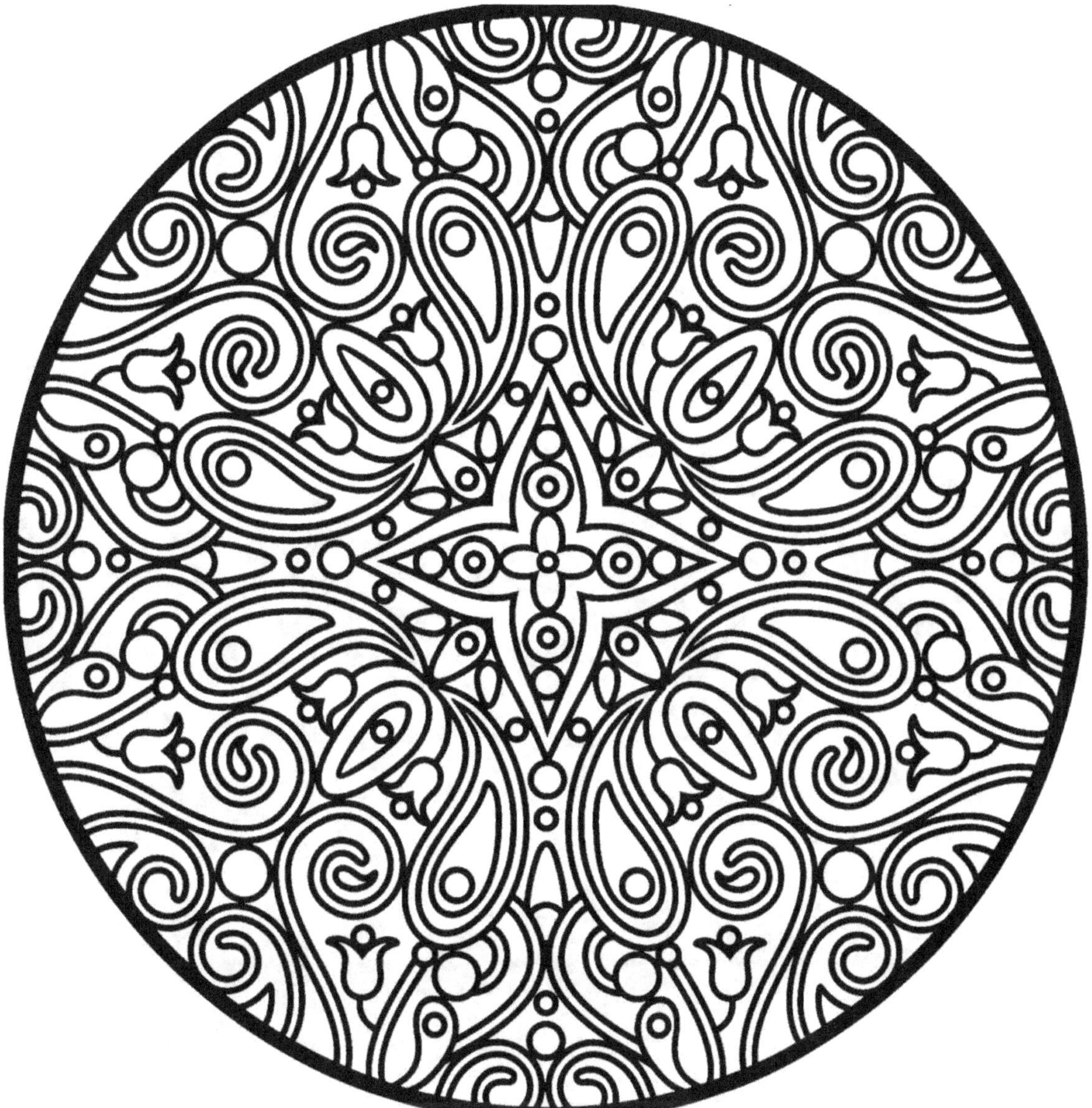

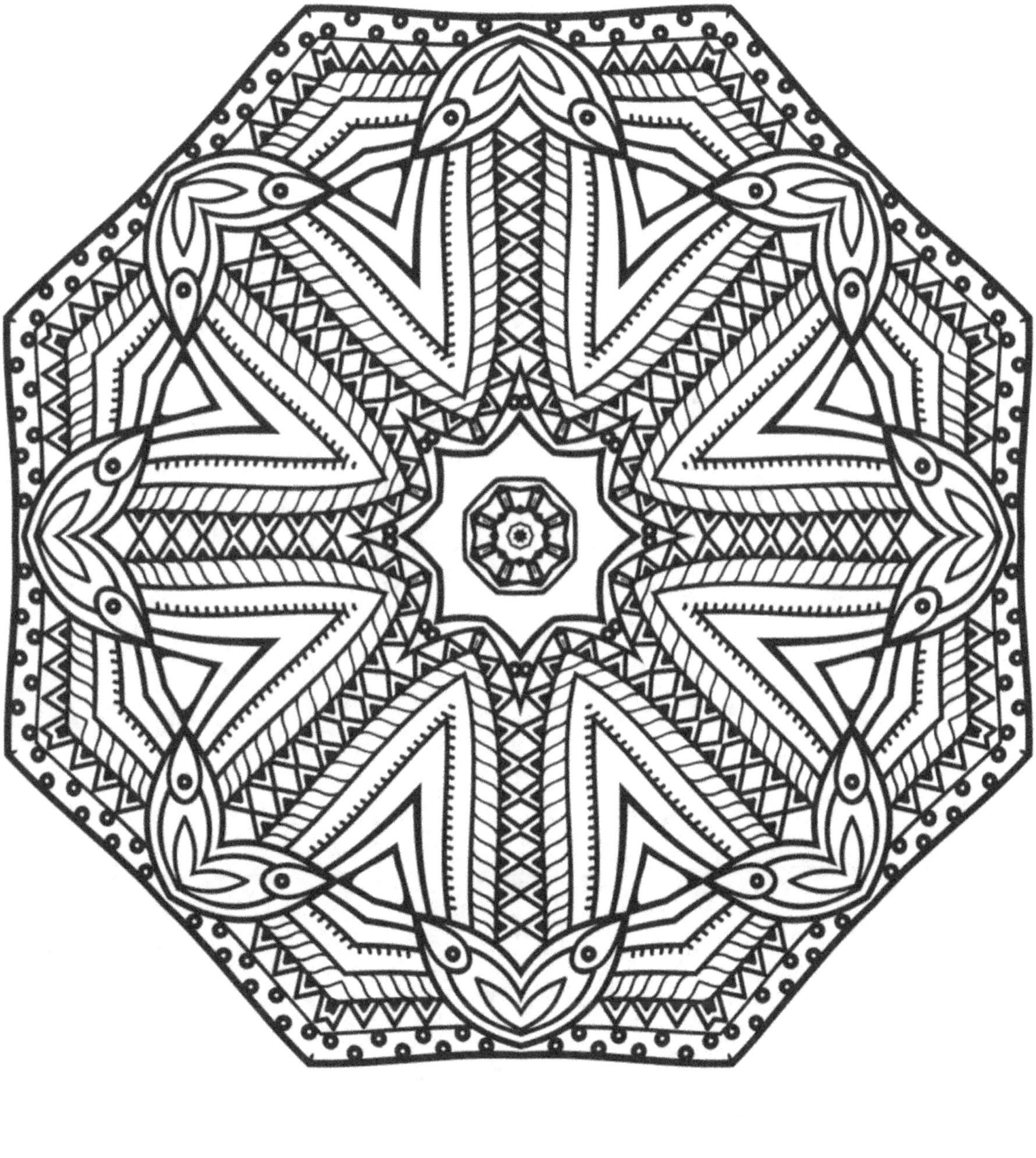

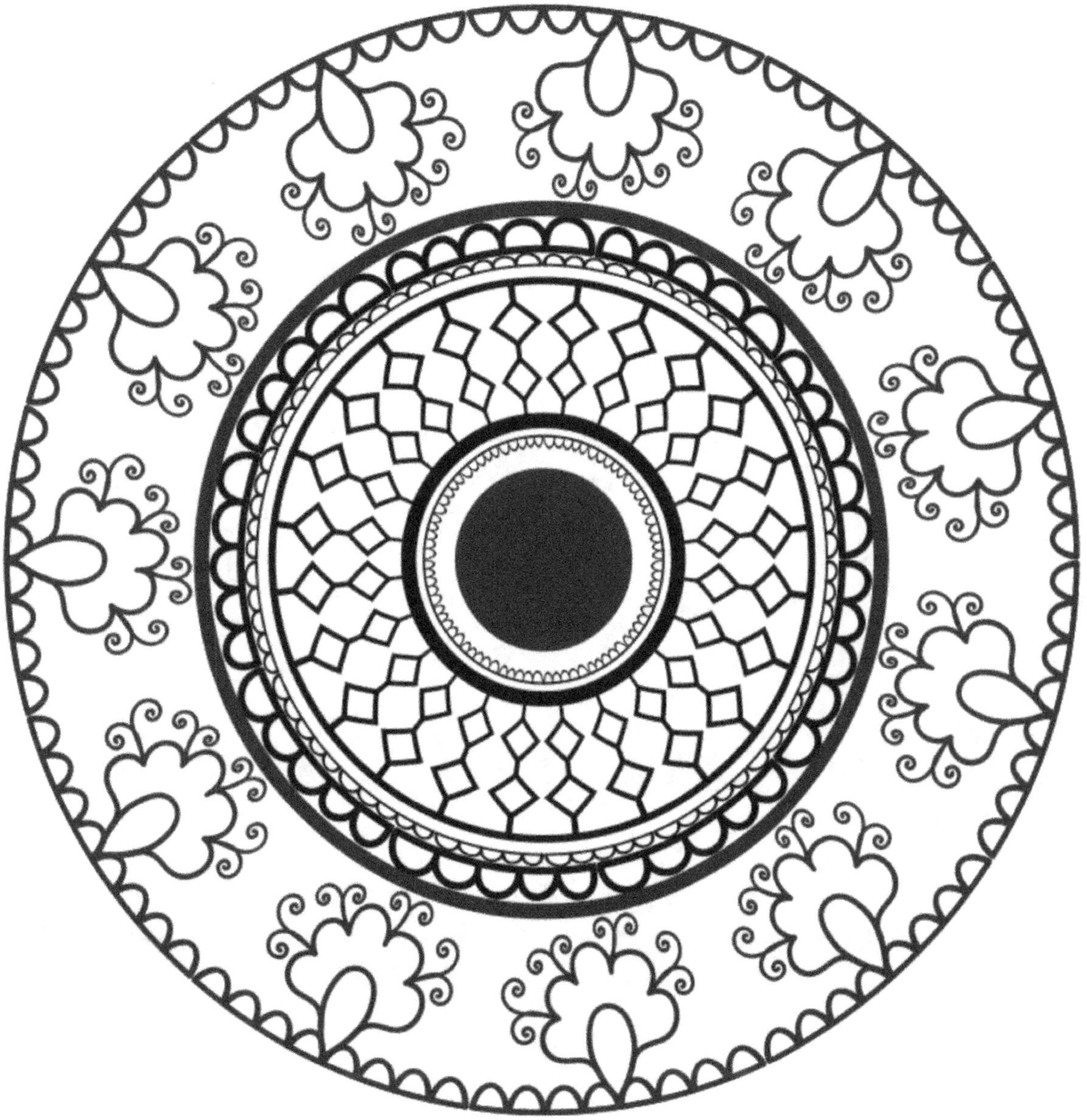

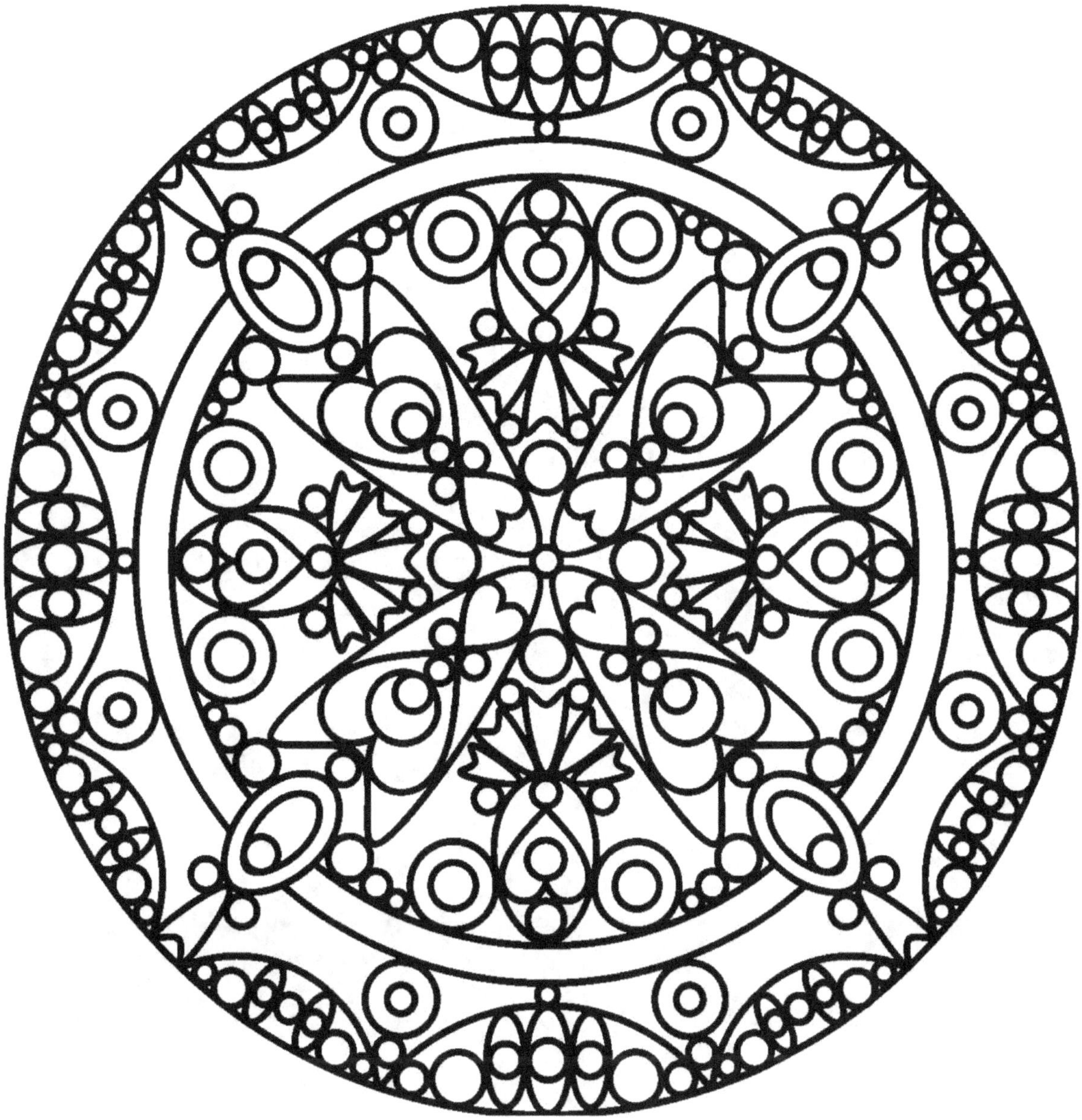

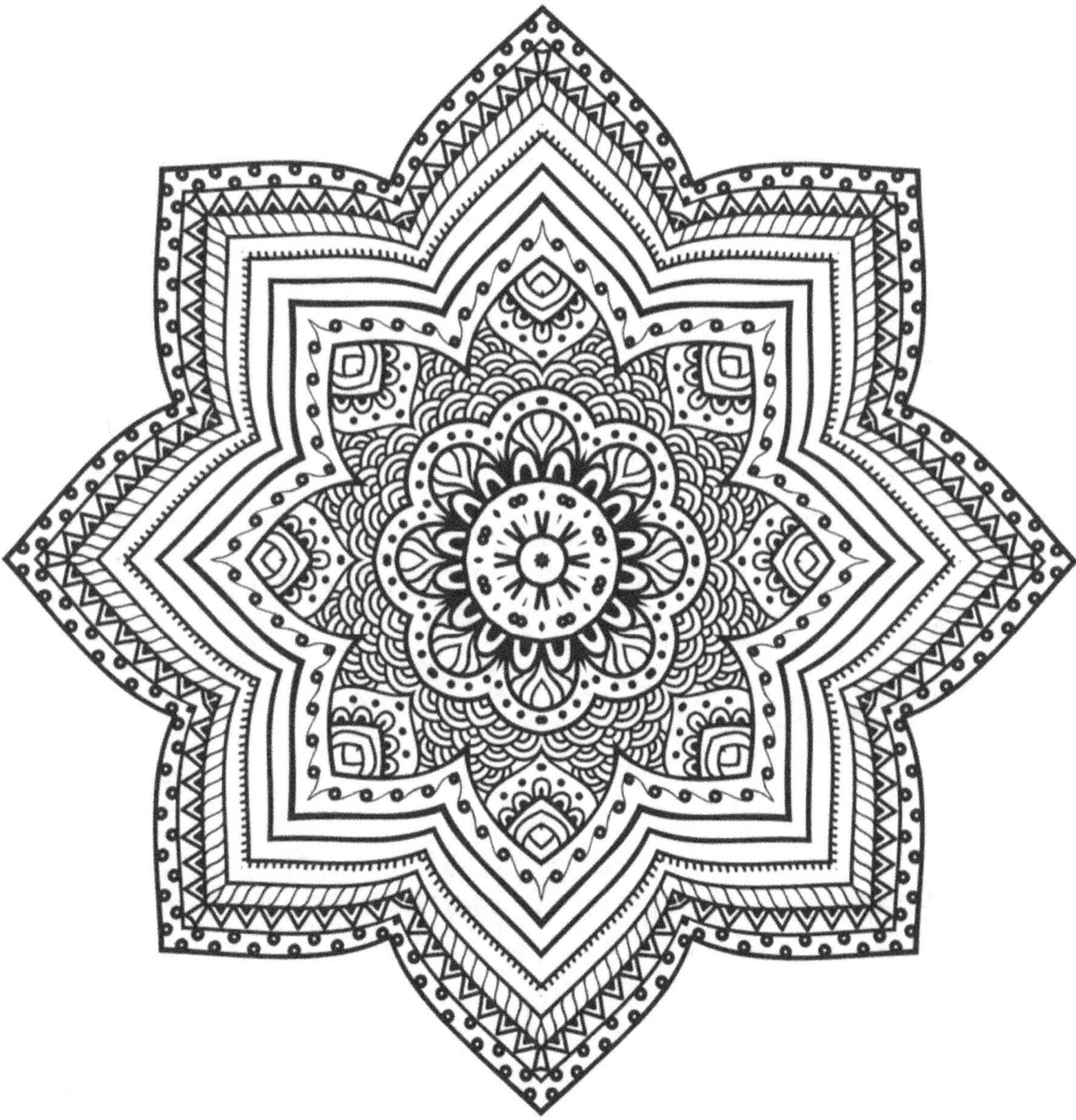

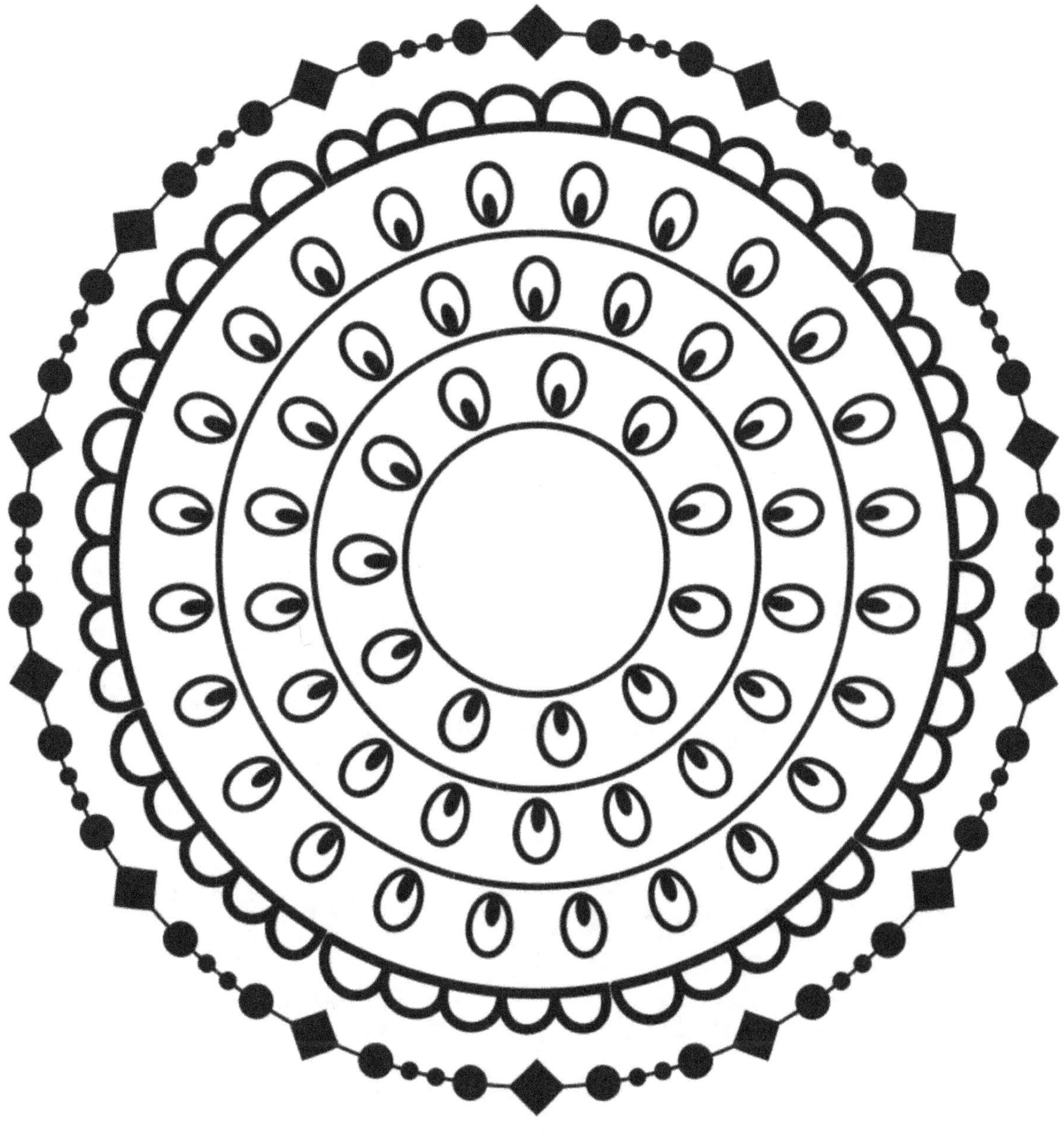

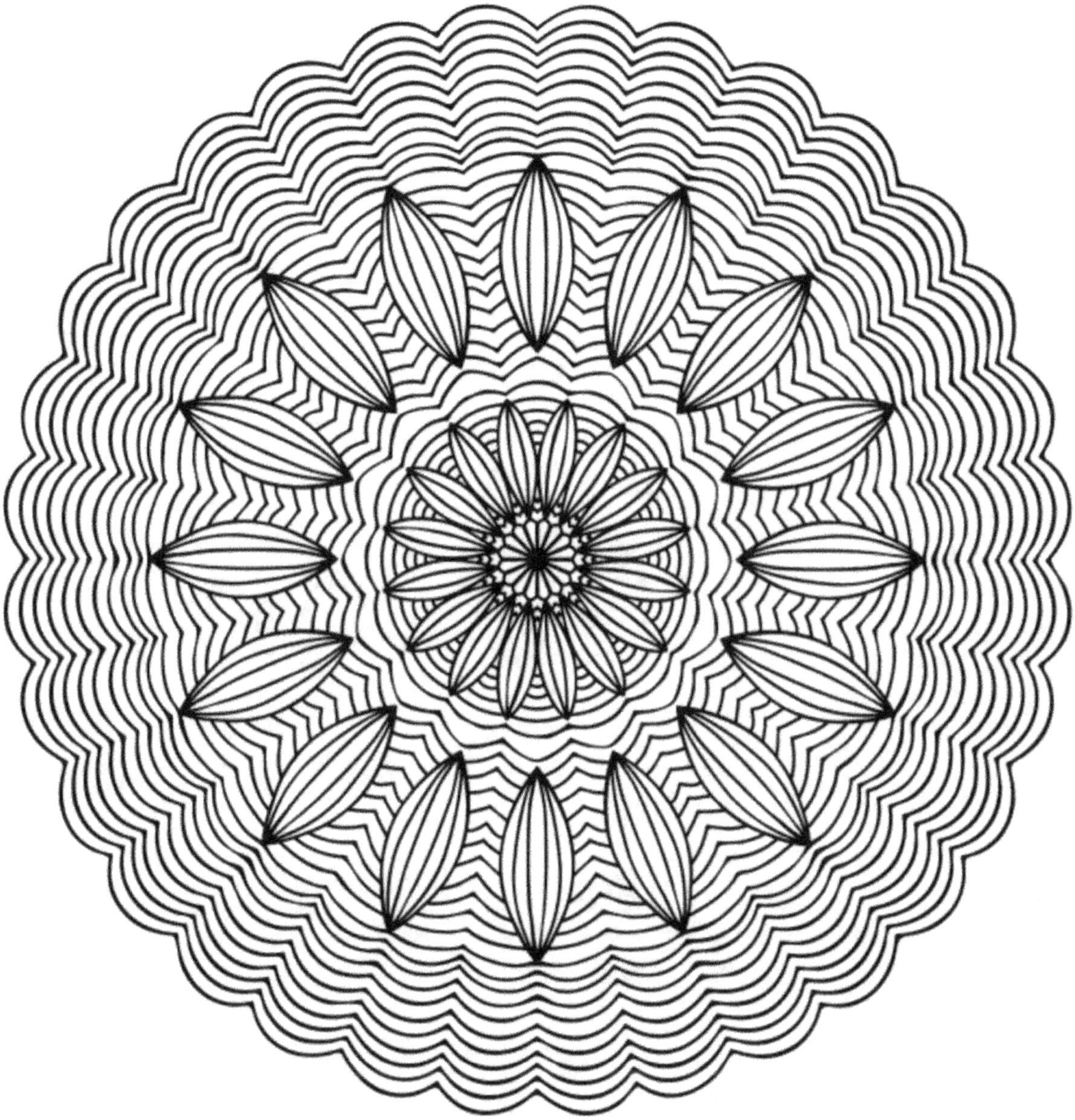

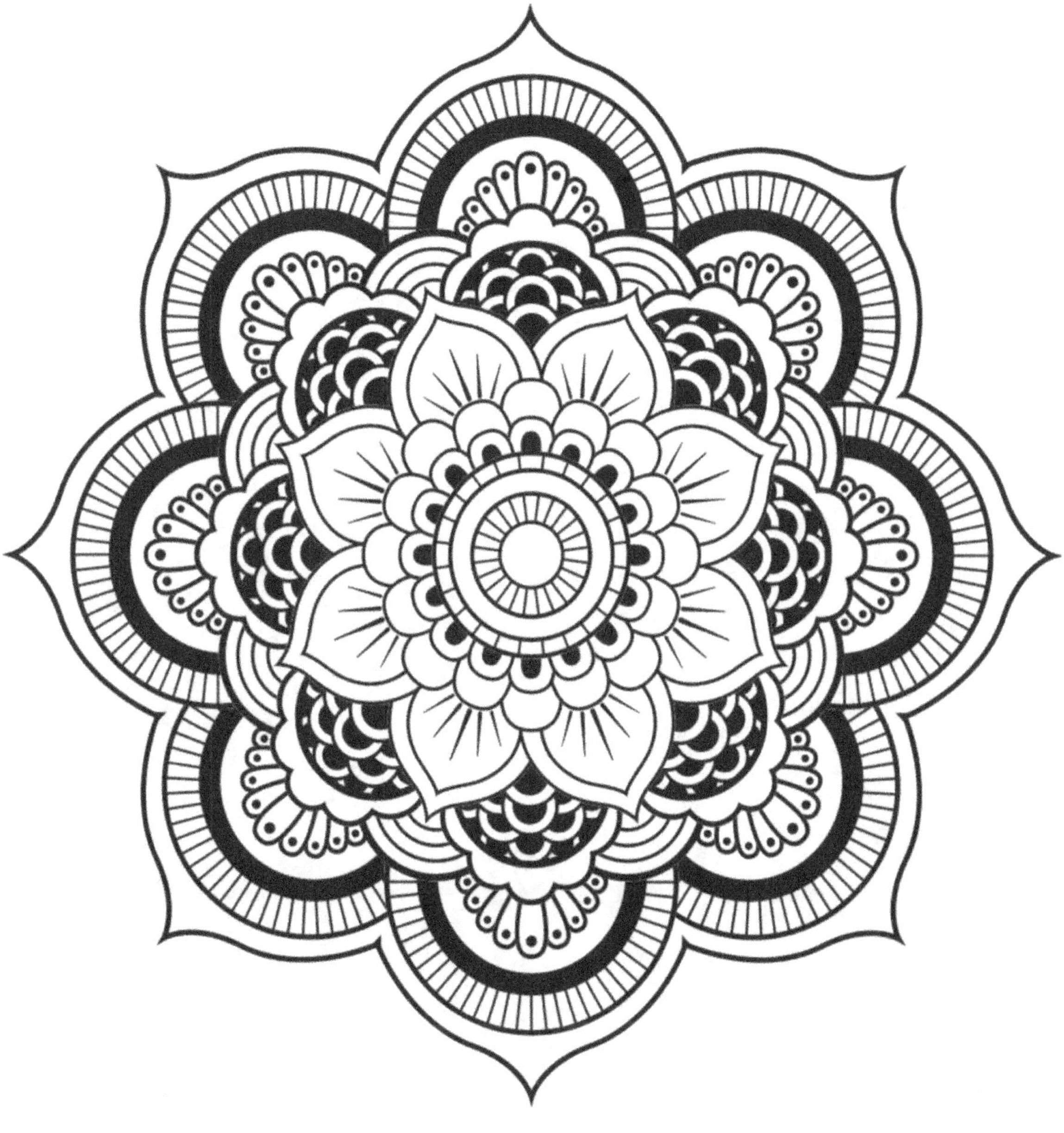

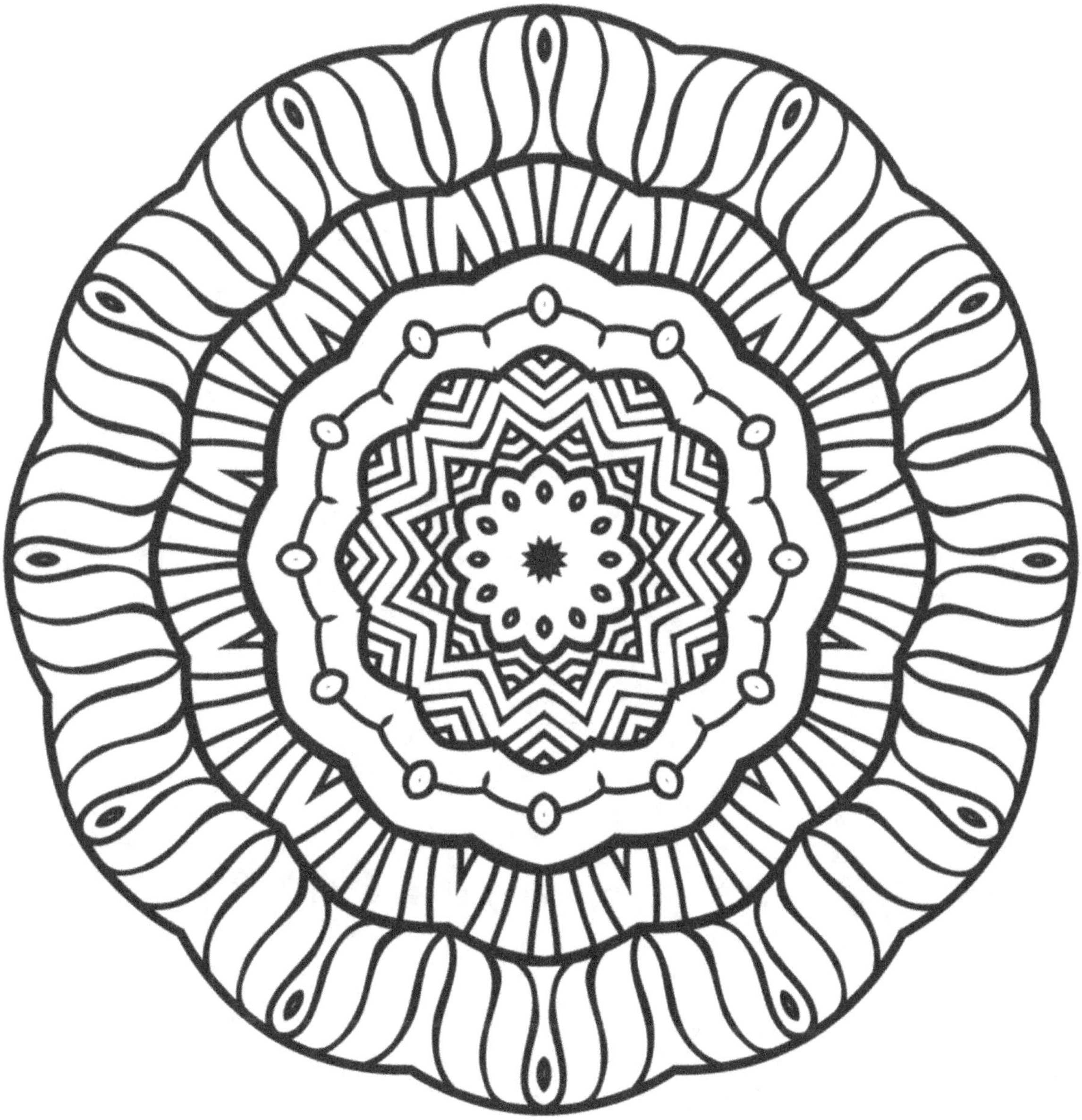

www.ingramcontent.com/pod-product-compliance
Lightning Source LLC
Chambersburg PA
CBHW080827180526
45168CB00006B/2598
* 9 7 8 1 5 1 5 1 9 4 0 2 6 *